Business Knowledge for IT in Investment Banking

A complete handbook for IT Professionals

UK Edition

Essvale Corporation Limited
The Forward Thinking Company

PROFESSIONAL SERIES

Essvale Corporation Limited
63 Apollo Building
1 Newton Place
London E14 3TS
www.essvale.com

This is the first edition of this publication.

Essvale Corporation Ltd is hereby identified as author
of this work in accordance with Section 77 of the
Copyright, Designs and Patents Act 1988

Requests to the authors should be addressed to:
permissions@essvale.com.

A CIP record for this book is available from the British Library

ISBN (10-digit) 0 95541 240 4
ISBN (13-digit) 978 0 95541 240 0

This publication is designed to provide accurate and authoritative
information about the subject matter. The author makes no representation,
express or implied, with regard to the accuracy of the information
contained in the publication and cannot accept any responsibility or
liability for any errors or omissions that it may contain.

Cover design by Essvale Design Team
Design and typesetting by Boldface, London EC1
Printed by Lightning Source Ltd, Milton Keynes

Preface

This is the maiden publication for the Business Knowledge for IT Professionals series that will include other exciting topics in the near future. The motivation for this publication is to bridge the gap in business knowledge between IT professionals and the business community. Readers will find the topics covered in this publication will get them up to speed with the knowledge they need to work in the exciting world of investment banking.

This publication covers topics including an overview of investment banking, the major players, products traded and so on. After reading this publication, readers will have the confidence to talk to the business users within investment banking, knowing that they have a firm grasp of what the business is all about. There will be future publications that delve deeper into the asset classes in investment banking such as Commodities, Equities, Fixed Income and Foreign Exchange and the mysterious hedge fund industry so readers that want to take their learning further should look out for other publications that deal with these subject areas.

The types of IT professional that would benefit from the knowledge in this publication include software developers, development managers, test analysts and managers already working in investment banking or those that would want to pursue a career in this industry. Other types are project managers, database administrators, support analysts and business analysts that are already working in investment banking or would like to cross over from other industries.

Undergraduates, post-graduates and those who have recently graduated can also benefit greatly from reading this publication.

Readers who feel that they would need instructor-led classes to support the knowledge gained from this manual should log on to www.essvale.com to browse the relevant courses and to register their details. In addition, we are going to launch a service to support this training initiative and the Bizle Professional Series publications on www.bizle.biz so readers are advised to check the Essvale website regularly to get details of when the service will be fully operational.

Finally, readers should please note that some of the data published is not up to date. This is as a result of our limitations in accessing data in some market segments such as hedge funds. The data in this publication is meant to be a guideline to the state of the markets and not a basis for extrapolation or forecasting.

Acknowledgements

Essvale Corporation Limited would like to thank all authors and publishers of all materials used in compiling this publication. Also thanks to all the respondents to the research carried out to justify writing this publication.

We would also like to acknowledge Lisa O'Reilly and Simon Barnaby of Royal Blue, Jennifer White of Calypso Inc., Severine Lopez of GL Trade, and Tatiana Liber of Sophis for their contribution to the chapter on systems in the investment banking sector.

Our thanks also go to Charlotte James of Sungard, Dorianne Landolphi of Openlink, Sebastian Matthews of Bursten Marstellar on behalf of SAP for Banking, and Kyle Arteaga, Elke Behrend, Albert Backburn and Steve Davies of Reuters. We also like to thank Paul Barry of IBM Consulting, Chris Gentle of Deloitte and all the helpful staff at the City Business Library in London. We need to acknowledge Barney Lodge, the designers at London Logo Company and ASK Translation, Pat Winfield of Bookworm Editorial Services, also Duncan James and Sue Kiel of Wiley Finance, Nikki Bannister of Pearson Finance and Shirley Davis on behalf of the IMF.

Contents

Introduction

These are exciting times for IT professionals; the business world has finally embraced IT as an integral part of the business. The IT industry is also maturing; it is becoming a recognised profession like law, accounting and engineering and there is a plethora of certifications out there to distinguish the IT professional. However, the training provided by corporations that hire IT professionals is inadequate in better integrating them into their business models. This situation needs to be addressed quickly to ensure that the banks can leverage the use of technology to deliver sustainable competitive advantage.

The idea behind this publication and others that will follow first came to the authors when they realised that there is a huge gulf in knowledge between the IT community and business, especially in the investment banking industry, as there is a wide range of products traded and the jargon involved is mind-boggling. After a series of interviews with IT professionals working in the industry and getting to grips with their frustration on the job, it was decided that a publication such as this had to be placed on the market as soon as possible.

Why is business knowledge of investment banking important?

IT professionals need to have knowledge of the investment banking industry for the following reasons:

- Investment banks need high-quality systems to ensure the smooth operation of the business.
- Business-critical IT projects in investment banks are executed to very aggressive deadlines and hence there is little provision for training IT professionals in the rudiments of the business justifications and implications of these projects.
- Errors in the output from IT systems can lead to fines from regulators.
- The future of IT demands that professionals have the specific industry knowledge to implement and support business-critical systems.
- The trends in the IT industry are changing the profession into a more specialised than generalised profession.
- Purely technical roles are increasingly outsourced to developing countries where labour costs are more competitive.
- To foster greater understanding between IT and the business with the benefit of creating more harmonised, multi-disciplinary project teams that will compress project timelines.

The benefits of an IT career in investment banking are enormous. Permanently employed IT professionals in investment banking can earn an average of 15%[*] more than their counterparts in other financial services companies and up to 20% more than other industries. Contractors on the other hand can earn up to

[*] Estimate based on the outcome of independent research.

40–50% more than their counterparts in other industries, depending on the area of investment banking they specialise in.

Furthermore, investment banks use the latest and most advanced relevant technology in their operations, so the relevantly skilled IT professional can be ahead of the pack in terms of technical ability. In fact, the industry is known to spend an inordinate amount on technology.

A career in investment banking also offers other benefits as follows:

- The opportunity to move from one bank to another as the business practices are almost identical.
- The opportunity to work in various locations across the world as some of the projects are part of global initiatives.
- The advantage of the location of the investment banks; they are usually centrally located in the West End, the City or Canary Wharf in London.
- The concentration of banks in these locations makes movement between them relatively easy.

The topics discussed in this publication were carefully selected to ensure a wide coverage of the theoretical underpinnings of the investment banking discipline as well as to demonstrate the alignment with IT. Business processes and tasks in the day-to-day activities of banking are mirrored in the associated business processes in IT systems, hence the necessity for the IT professional to have a firm grasp of these activities.

This publication is targeted at the UK market and as such the practices described are primarily UK focused. However, as the financial markets are global in nature, some aspects are discussed in a global context.

Overview of Investment Banking

1

This chapter introduces the concept of investment banking, the business functions and a list of notable investment banks.

Introduction

Investment banks can be described as multifaceted financial institutions that engage in public and private market transactions for corporations, governments and investors and also provide strategic advisory services. These transactions include mergers, acquisitions, underwriting of securities and divestitures. They also act as intermediaries in trading for clients. Investment banks differ from commercial banks, which take deposits and make commercial and retail loans. In recent years, however, the lines between the two types of structures have blurred, especially as commercial banks have offered more investment banking services. In the US, the Glass-Steagall Act, initially created in the wake of the Stock Market Crash of 1929, prohibited banks from both accepting deposits and underwriting securities; Glass-Steagall was repealed by the Gramm-Leach-Bliley Act in 1998. Investment banks may also differ from brokerages, which in general assist in the purchase and sale of stocks, bonds, and mutual funds. However, some firms operate as both brokerages and investment banks; these include some of the best known financial services firms in the world.

Definition of Investment Bank

An institution which acts as an underwriter or agent for corporations and municipalities issuing securities. Most also maintain broker/dealer operations, maintain markets for previously issued securities, and offer advisory services to investors. Investment banks also have a large role in facilitating mergers and acquisitions, private equity placements and corporate restructuring. (Investorwords.com)

The term "investment banking" tends to be used these days as something of an encompassing expression for a set of more-or-less related activities in the world of finance. Firms such as Merrill Lynch or Goldman Sachs are 'pure' investments banks whilst others like HSBC and Citigroup are universal banks with commercial and investment banking subsidiaries.

There appears to be considerable confusion today about what does and does not constitute an "investment bank" and "investment banker". In the strictest definition, investment banking is the raising of funds; both in debt and equity, and the name of the division handling this in an investment bank is often called the "Investment Banking Division" (IBD). However, only a few small boutique firms solely provide this – such as Crosby Capital – with almost all investment banks heavily involved in providing additional financial services for clients such as the trading of fixed income, foreign exchange, commodity and equity securities. It is therefore acceptable to refer to both the "Investment Banking Division" and other "front office" divisions, such as "Fixed Income", as part of "investment banking", and any employee involved in either side an "investment banker".

Role of modern Investment Banks

The original purpose of an investment bank was to raise capital and advise on mergers and acquisitions and other corporate financial strategies. As banking firms have diversified, investment banks have come to fill a variety of roles (list taken from the Swiss Banking Institute) such as:

- underwriting, syndicating and distributing new security issues;
- offering brokerage services to public & institutional investors;
- providing financial advice to corporate clients, especially on security issues, M&A deals;
- providing financial security research to investors and corporate customers;
- market-making, in particular securities.

Investment banks have also moved into foreign exchange markets, private banking, asset management and bridge financing.

Raising Capital in the Capital Markets

A key role of investment banks is to help companies raise capital in the capital markets by arranging the issuance of new securities. There are two ways to do this: through a public offering or through a private placement.

A public offering involves selling securities to a wide range of investors. The investment bank can sell the company's stock in an initial public offering or secondary offering, or they can arrange a bond issue. As these securities can end up with many investors, including unsophisticated ones, these sales are tightly regulated by bodies such as the Financial Services Authority.

A "private placement" is an offering of securities to a small group of sophisticated investors. There are fewer rules to comply with, though the investment bank must show that the investors comply with certain criteria. The distribution of other types of investment, other than securities, is usually also done through a private placement. This could include investments in venture capital or private equity, acquisitions and other strategic investments by companies.

The main Activities and Units

Large global investment banks typically have several business units, including Investment Banking, concerned with advising public and private corporations: Research, concerned with producing reports on valuations of financial products; and Sales and Trading, concerned with buying and selling products both on behalf of the bank's clients and also for the bank itself. Banks undertake risk through Proprietary Trading, done by a special set of traders who do not interface with clients and through Principal Risk, risk undertaken by traders after they

3

buy or sell a product to a client and do not hedge their total exposure. Banks seek to maximise profitability for a given amount of risk on their balance sheet.

An investment bank is split into the so-called Front Office, Middle Office and Back Office, with Front Office widely deemed as having the highest-calibre employees in terms of intellectual and/or interpersonal capital, and Back Office the least. The individual activities are described below.

Front Office

■ Investment Banking is the traditional aspect of investment banks which involves helping customers raise funds in the Capital Markets and advising on mergers and acquisitions. Investment bankers prepare idea pitches that they bring to meetings with their clients, with the expectation that their efforts will be rewarded with a mandate when the client is ready to undertake a transaction. Once mandated, an investment bank is responsible for preparing all materials necessary for the transaction as well as the execution of the deal, which may involve subscribing investors to a security issuance, coordinating with bidders, or negotiating with a merger target. Other terms for the Investment Banking Division include Mergers & Acquisitions (M&A) and Corporate Finance.

■ Financial Markets is split into the four key divisions of Sales, Trading, Research and Structuring:

   ■ *Sales and Trading* – often the most profitable area of an investment bank, responsible for the majority of revenue of most investment banks. In the process of market making, traders will buy and sell financial products with the goal of making an incremental amount of money on each trade. Sales is the term for the investment bank's sales force, whose primary job is to call on institutional and high-net-worth investors to suggest trading ideas (on a caveat emptor basis) and take orders. Sales desks then communicate their clients' orders to the appropriate trading desks, which can price and execute trades, or structure new products that fit a specific need.

   ■ *Research* – the division which reviews companies and writes reports about their prospects, often with "buy" or "sell" ratings. While the research division generates no revenue, its resources are used to assist traders in trading, the sales force in suggesting ideas to customers, and investment bankers by covering their clients. In recent years the relationship between investment banking and research has become highly regulated, reducing its importance to the investment bank.

   ■ *Structuring* – has been a relatively recent division as Derivatives have come into play, with highly technical and numerate employees working on creating complex structured products which typically offer much greater margins and returns than underlying cash securities.

Middle Office

■ Risk Management involves analysing the risk that traders are taking onto the balance sheet in conducting their daily trades, and setting limits on the amount of capital that they are able to trade in order to prevent "bad" trades having a detrimental effect on a desk overall.

Back Office
▓ Operations involve data-checking trades that have been conducted, ensuring that they are not erroneous, and transacting the required transfers. Whilst it provides the greatest job security of divisions within an investment bank, it is widely known to involve the most monotonous work at relatively low pay.
▓ Technology – every major investment bank has considerable amounts of in-house software, created by the Technology team, who are also responsible for Computer and Telecommunications-based support.

Recent Evolution of the Business

Investment Banking is constantly evolving. One main course of evolution is with investment banking products. Investment banks constantly invent new products, which are usually accompanied by very high profit margins since buyers are not sure how to value them. However, since these cannot be patented or copyrighted, they are very often copied quickly by other investment banks, and margins are forced downward as the pricing approaches commodity pricing. Throughout investment banking history, many have theorised that all investment banking products and services would be commoditised, and the concentration of power in the bulge bracket would be eliminated. This has failed to happen because, while many products became commoditised, new ones were constantly being invented. For example, trading stocks for customers is now a commodity-style business, but creating stock derivative contracts is now a very high margin business since the contracts are difficult to evaluate. In addition, while many products have been commoditised, an increasing amount of investment bank profit has come from proprietary trading, where size creates a positive network benefit (since the more trades an investment bank does, the more it knows about the market, allowing it theoretically to make better trades).

Possible Conflicts of Interest
Potential conflicts of interest may arise between different parts of a bank, creating the potential for financial movements that could be deemed as market manipulation. Authorities that regulate investment banking, like the Financial Services Authority, require that banks impose a Chinese wall, which prohibits communication between Investment Banking on one side and Research and Equities on the other.

Some of the conflicts of interest involved in investment banking are listed here.

▓ Historically, equity research firms were founded and owned by investment banks. One common practice is for equity analysts to initiate coverage on a company in order to develop relationships that lead to highly profitable investment banking business. In the 1990s, many equity researchers alleg-edly traded positive stock ratings directly for investment banking business. On the flip side of the coin, companies would threaten to divert investment banking business to competitors unless their stock was rated favourably. Politicians acted to pass laws to criminalise such acts. Increased pressure from regulators and a series of lawsuits, settlements and prosecutions curbed this business to a large extent following the 2001 stock market tumble.

- Many investment banks also own retail brokerages. Also during the 1990s, some retail brokerages sold consumers securities which did not meet their stated risk profile. This behaviour may have led to investment banking busi-ness or even sales of surplus shares during a public offering to keep public perception of the stock favourable.
- Since investment banks engage heavily in trading for their own account, there is always the temptation or possibility that they might engage in some form of front running.

Boutique Investment Banks

What is a Boutique Investment Bank?

A boutique investment bank is a bank that offers a narrow range of services and to be independent it should not be part of a larger financial institution that serves many competitive and potentially conflicting interests.

Overview of Boutique Investment Banking

A boutique investment bank's focus is on advisory work. It has no research, trad-ing, lending or related activities. Instead it remains dedicated to providing con-flict-free and client-focused advice. The focus is solely on clients' needs and its energies are devoted to offering solutions without the distraction of trading, underwriting or publishing research and the impact its advice will have other parts of its organisation.

Boutique investment banks, in focusing on providing advice, tend to use third-party providers to complete deals. For example, an initial public offering will require the use of one or many brokerage firms and some deals may involve the raising of the bank debt. The boutique bank, based on its knowledge and experience, can source the best providers of these services and create competi-tive advantage between the bidders.

List of some Investment Banks

Some notable public and private investment banks and financial services firms that have investment banking business in the UK include:

- Abbey Financial markets
- ABN AMRO

- Bank of America
- Bank of New York
- The Bank of Tokyo-Mitsubishi UFJ
- Barclays Capital
- Bear Stearns
- BNP Paribas
- Cazenove
- CIBC World Markets
- Citigroup
- Commerze Bank
- Credit Lyonnais
- Credit Suisse
- Daiwa
- Deutsche Bank.

Others are:

- Dresdner Kleinwort Wasserstein
- Goldman Sachs
- ING
- JP Morgan Chase
- Lazard
- Lehman Brothers
- Merrill Lynch
- Mizuho Corporate Bank
- Morgan Stanley
- Nomura
- Rabo Bank
- RBC Capital Markets
- Rothschild
- RBS Financial Markets
- Societe General Bank
- UBS
- West LB Panmure.

Asset Classes in Investment Banking

*This chapter describes the different asset classes,
the markets in which they are traded,
the security identifier types and indices.*

Introduction

What is an Asset Class?

An asset class is a specific category of assets or investments, such as stocks, bonds, cash and currency. There have been more liberal definitions of asset classes in recent times and an example is as follows: "If it moves up and down independently then it is an asset class."

Asset classes in investment banking are usually categorised into the following:

- foreign exchange
- fixed income
- equities
- commodities
- cash.

Foreign Exchange

Foreign exchange is traded in a global technology-based marketplace in which banks, corporations, governments and institutional investors trade currencies around the clock. The foreign exchange market is the largest market in the world, in terms of cash value traded.

Common Foreign Exchange Instruments

- spot
- outward forward trades
- currency options
- currency futures
- foreign exchange swaps
- non-deliverable forwards.

Foreign Exchange Market Size and Liquidity

The foreign exchange market is unique because of:

- its trading volume;
- the extreme liquidity of the market;
- the large number of, and variety of, traders in the market;
- its geographical dispersion;
- its long trading hours – 24 hours a day (except on weekends);
- the variety of factors that affect exchange rates.

Average daily international foreign exchange trading volume was $1.9 trillion in April 2004 according to the Bank of International Settlements study. The breakdown is as follows:

- $600 billion spot
- $1,300 billion in derivatives, i.e.:
    - $200 billion in outright forwards
    - $1,000 billion in foreign exchange swaps
    - $100 billion in currency options.

The bulk of these deals are done by the likes of Citigroup, HSBC, and Deutsche bank. These banks facilitate the trading and investment activities of their corporate and institutional clients by standing ready to lend or exchange a wide range of currencies, and in turn make markets in currencies amongst themselves.

The banks continually provide the market with both bid (buy) and ask (sell) prices. The bid/ask spread is the difference between the price at which a bank will sell ("ask", or "offer") and the price at which a market-maker will buy ("bid") from a wholesale customer.

Trading Characteristics

There is no single unified foreign exchange market. Owing to the over-the-counter (OTC) nature of currency markets, there are rather a number of interconnected marketplaces, where different currency instruments are traded. This implies that there is no such thing as a single dollar rate, but rather a number of different rates (prices), depending on what bank or market-maker is trading. In practice the rates are often very close, otherwise they could be exploited by arbitrageurs.

The main trading centres are in London, New York, and Tokyo, but banks throughout the world participate. As the Asian trading session ends, the European session begins, and then the US session, and then the Asian begin in their turn. Traders can react to news when it breaks, rather than waiting for the market to open.

There is little or no "inside information" in the foreign exchange markets. Exchange rate fluctuations are usually caused by actual monetary flows as well as by expectations of changes in monetary flows caused by changes in GDP growth, inflation, interest rates, budget and trade deficits or surpluses, and other macroeconomic conditions. Major news is released publicly, often on scheduled dates; so many people have access to the same news at the same time.

Currencies are traded against one another. Each pair of currencies thus constitutes an individual product and is traditionally noted XXX/YYY, where YYY is the ISO 4217 international three-letter code of the currency into which the price of one unit of XXX currency is expressed. For instance, EUR/USD is the price of the euro expressed in US dollars, as in 1 euro = 1.2045 dollars.

On the spot market, according to the BIS study, the most heavily traded products were:

- EUR/USD – 28 %
- USD/JPY – 17 %
- GBP/USD (also called *cable*) – 14 %.

Table 2.1 Characteristics of the most commonly traded currencies

Rank	Currency	ISO	Symbol
1	United States Dollar	USD	$
2	Eurozone Euro	EUR	€
3	Japanese Yen	JPY	¥
4	British Pound Sterling	GBP	£

And the US currency was involved in 89% of transactions, followed by the euro (37%), the yen (20%) and sterling (17%). Although trading in the euro has grown considerably since the currency's creation in January 1999, the foreign exchange market is thus still largely dollar-centred. For instance, trading the euro versus a non-European currency ZZZ will usually involve two trades: EUR/USD and USD/ZZZ. The only exception to this is EUR/JPY, which is an established traded currency pair in the interbank spot market.

Market Participants

According to the Bank for International Settlements' last triennial study (April 2004) (Triennial Central Bank Survey of Foreign Exchange and Derivatives Market Activity 2004 – Final Results), transactions:

- were strictly interdealer (i.e. interbank) for 53 %;
- for 33% involved a dealer (i.e. a bank) and a fund manager or some other non-bank financial institution;
- for only 14 % were between a dealer and a non-financial company.

Fixed Income

Fixed income refers to any type of investment that yields a regular (fixed) payment. For example, if you borrow money and have to pay interest once a month, you have issued a fixed income security. When a company does this, it is called a bond. Fixed Income departments in most banks engage mainly in bond trading but in some banks they also trade in money market instruments.

The Money Market is the market for short-term borrowing and lending, typically up to one year. In the money markets, banks lend to and borrow from each other short-term financial instruments such as certificates of deposit (CDs) or enter into agreements such as repurchase agreements (repos). It provides short- to medium-term liquidity in the global financial system.

Bonds

A bond is a debt security in which the issuer owes the holder a debt and is obliged to repay the principal and interest (the coupon). Other stipulations may also be attached to the bond issue, such as the obligation for the issuer to provide certain information to the bond holder, or limitations on the behaviour of

11

the issuer. Bonds are generally issued for a fixed term (the maturity) longer than one year.

Bonds and stocks (equity) are both securities, but the difference is that stock holders own a part of the issuing company (have an equity stake), whereas bond holders are in essence lenders to the issuer. Also bonds have a definite lifespan, their maturity, whereas stocks may be held indefinitely.

Trading Characteristics

In some markets such as the UK, France and Germany, government bonds are listed on the local stock exchange. However, in these and most countries including the US, government bonds are traded mainly in the over-the-counter (OTC) markets through dealers in the banks. Dealers support the liquidity of the market by making the bid (buy) and offer or ask (sell) prices. Their prices are displayed on screen-based information services such as Bloomberg and deals are contracted over the phone or electronic communication.

Market Size

The largest government bond market in the world is the market for the US government debt, followed by the government bond markets in Japan, Italy and Germany.

Issuers

The range of issuers of bonds is very large. Almost any organisation could issue bonds, but the underwriting and legal costs can be prohibitive. Regulations to issue bonds are very strict. Issuers are often classified as follows:

- Supranational agencies, such as the European Investment Bank or the Asian Development Bank issue supranational bonds.
- National Governments issue Government bonds in their own currency. These are often called risk-free bonds. They also issue sovereign bonds in foreign currencies.
- Companies (corporates) issue corporate bonds.
- Special-purpose vehicles are companies set up for the sole purpose of containing assets against which bonds are issued, often asset-backed securities.

Issuing Bonds

Bonds are issued by governments or other public authorities, credit institutions, companies and supranational institutions in the primary markets. The most common process of issuing bonds is through underwriting. One or more banks, forming a syndicate, underwrite the bonds and sell them on to their customers. Government bonds are typically auctioned. Bonds enable the issuer to finance long-term investments with external funds.

Features of Bonds

The most important features of a bond are:

- *Nominal, principal or face amount* – the amount over which the issuer pays interest and which has to be repaid at the end.
- *Issue price* – the price at which investors buy the bonds when they are first issued. The net proceeds that the issuer receives are calculated as the issue price, less the fees for the underwriters, times the nominal amount.
- *Maturity date* – the date on which the issuer has to repay the nominal amount. After the maturity date the issuer has no more obligations to the bond holders, as long as all payments have been made of course. The length of time until the maturity date is often referred to as the term or simply maturity of a bond. The maturity can be any length of time, although debt securities with a term of less than one year are generally designated money-market instruments rather than bonds. Most bonds have a term of up to 30 years. Some bonds have been issued with maturities of up to 100 years, and some even do not mature at all. These are called perpetuities. In early 2005, a market developed in euros for bonds with a maturity of 50 years.
- *Coupon* – the interest rate that the issuer pays to the bond holders. Usually this rate is fixed throughout the life of the bond. It can also vary with a money-market index, such as LIBOR, or it can be even more exotic. The name coupon originates from the fact that in the past, physical bonds were issued which had coupons attached to them. On coupon dates the bond holder would give the coupon to a bank in exchange for the interest payment.
- *Coupon dates* – the dates on which the issuer pays the coupon to the bond holders. In the US, most bonds are semi-annual, which means that they pay a coupon every six months. In Europe, most bonds are annual and pay only one coupon a year.
- *Callability* – some bonds give the issuer the right to repay the bond before the maturity date on the call dates. These bonds are referred to as callable bonds. Most callable bonds allow the issuer to repay the bond at par. With some bonds the issuer has to pay a premium, the so-called call premium. This is mainly the case for high-yield bonds. These have very strict covenants, restricting the issuer in its operations. To be free from these covenants, the issuer can repay the bonds early, but only at a high cost.
- *Puttability* – some bonds give the bond holder the call dates, usually coinciding with coupon dates.
- *European callable right* – a right to force the issuer to repay the bond before the maturity date on the put dates.
- *Call dates and put dates* – the dates on which callable and puttable bonds can be redeemed early. There are four main categories:
  - A Bermudan callable has several call dates, usually coinciding with coupon dates.
  - The European callable has only one call date. This is a special case of a Bermudan callable.
  - An American callable can be called at any time until the maturity date.
  - A Death Put – an optional redemption feature on a debt instrument allowing the beneficiary of the estate of the deceased to put (sell) the

13

bond (back to the issuer) in the event of the beneficiary's death or legal incapacitation. Also known as a "survivor's option".

■ *Indenture* – a document specifying the rights of bond holders. In the US, federal and state securities and commercial laws apply to the enforcement of these documents, which are construed by courts as contracts. The terms may be changed while the bonds are outstanding but amendments to the governing document often require approval by a majority vote of the bond holders.

Types of Bonds

■ *Fixed-rate bonds* – bonds with a coupon that remains constant throughout the life of the bond.

■ *Floating-rate notes (FRNs)* – bonds that have a coupon that is linked to a money-market index, such as LIBOR or EURIBOR, for example three months USD LIBOR +0.20%. The coupon is then reset periodically, normally every three months.

■ *Convertible bonds* – bonds that can be converted, on the maturity date, into another kind of security, usually common stock in the company that issued the bonds.

■ *High-yield bonds* – bonds that are rated below investment grade by the credit rating agencies. As these bonds are relatively risky, investors expect to earn a higher yield, hence the name high-yield bonds. Those market participants that want to emphasise the risky nature of the bonds also call them junk bonds.

■ *Zero coupon bonds* – bonds that do not pay any interest. They trade at a substantial discount from par. The bond holder receives the full principal amount on the maturity date. An example of zero coupon bonds is Series E savings bonds issued by the US Government. Zero coupon bonds may be created from fixed-rate bonds by financial institutions by "stripping off" the coupons. In other words, the coupons are separated from the final principal payment of the bond and traded independently.

■ *Inflation-linked bonds* – a bond in which the principal amount is indexed to inflation. The interest rate is lower than for fixed-rate bonds with a comparable maturity. However, as the principal amount grows, the payments increase with inflation. The government of the United Kingdom was the first to issue inflation-linked Gilts in the 1980s. Treasury Inflation-Protected Securities (TIPS) and I-bonds are examples of inflation-linked bonds issued by the US Government.

■ *Asset-backed securities* – bonds whose interest and principal payments are backed by underlying cash flows from other assets. Examples of asset-backed securities are mortgage-backed securities (MBS), collateralised mortgage obligations (CMO) and collateralised debt obligations (CDO).

■ *Perpetual bonds* – often called perpetuities. They have no maturity date. The most famous of these are the UK Consols, which are also known as Treasury Annuities or Undated Treasuries. Some of these were issued back in 1888 and still trade today.

Money Markets Instruments
Trading of money markets instruments takes place between banks in the "money centres" (New York and London primarily, also Chicago, Frankfurt, Paris, Singapore, Hong Kong, Tokyo, Toronto, Sydney).

Common Money Markets Instruments
- *Bankers' acceptance* – A draft or bill of exchange accepted by a bank to guarantee payment of the bill.
- *Certificate of deposit* – A time deposit with a specific maturity date shown on a certificate; large-denomination certificates of deposits can be sold before maturity.
- *Commercial paper* – An unsecured promissory note with a fixed maturity of 1 to 270 days; usually it is sold at a discount from face value.
- *Eurodollar deposit* – Dollar deposits in a US bank branch or a non-US bank located outside the United States.
- *Repurchase agreements (repos)* – Short-term loans – normally for less than two weeks and frequently for one day – arranged by selling securities to an investor with an agreement to repurchase them at a fixed price on a fixed date.
- *Treasury bills* – Short-term debt obligations of a national government that are issued to mature in 3 to 12 months.
- *Forward Rate Agreement (FRA)* – a forward contract in which one party pays a fixed interest rate and receives a floating interest rate equal to a reference rate (the underlying rate).

Commodities

Investment banks trade in the commodity markets i.e. a market where raw or primary products are exchanged.

Definition of Commodities
A basic agricultural, mineral or other basic product traded on a commodity exchange.

What is a Commodity Exchange?
A commodity exchange is an organisation typically owned by its trading members, organised to facilitate bringing buyers and sellers of various commodities, or their agents, together to foster spot or futures trading in specified commodities.

The following are different categories of commodities that banks trade in:

- precious metals;
- foodstuffs;
- base metals.

Table 2.2 List of some precious metals

Commodity	Unit	Exchange
Gold	Troy ounce	OTC London Bullion Market
Silver	Troy ounce	OTC London Bullion Market
Platinum	Troy ounce	OTC London Platinum Market

Table 2.3 List of some foodstuffs

Commodity	Unit	Exchange
Sugar	1000kg	London Commodity Exchange
Cocoa	1000kg	London Commodity Exchange
Wheat	100kg	London Commodity Exchange

Table 2.4 List of some base metals

Commodity	Unit	Exchange
Copper	1000kg	London Metals Exchange
Lead	1000kg	London Metals Exchange
Aluminium	1000kg	London Metals Exchange

Commonly Traded Commodity Instruments

Energy
Crude Oil Options:
- Heating Oil Futures
- Natural Gas Future
- Electricity Futures

Metal:
- Copper Futures
- Aluminium Futures
- Lead Options

Foodstuffs:
- Sugar Options
- Wheat Futures
- Cocoa Futures

Equities

Equities trading, in investment banking, covers trading of Primary Equity and Equity Derivatives aimed at corporate customers. Equity investment, on the other hand, generally refers to the buying and holding of shares of stock on a stock market by individuals and funds in anticipation of income from dividends and capital gain as the value of the stock rises.

Definition
Equity is ordinary shares or common stock i.e. shareholding of a company whereby dividends are paid to the holders if the company makes a profit, and/or participation in the growth in value of the company.

Types of Shares
There are several types of shares, including common stock, preferred stock, treasury stock and dual class shares. Preferred stock, sometimes called preference shares, has priority over common stock in the distribution of dividends and assets, and sometimes has enhanced voting rights such as the ability to veto mergers or acquisitions or the right of first refusal when new shares are issued (i.e. the holder of the preferred stock can buy as much as they want before the stock is offered to others). A dual class equity structure has several classes of shares (for example Class A, Class B, and Class C) each with its own advantages and disadvantages. Treasury stocks are shares that have been bought back from the public. Treasury Stock is considered issued but not outstanding.

The Equity Market
The equity market is broadly divided into primary and secondary markets. The primary market is one in which securities are sold for the first time. A secondary market is one in which existing securities are traded.

An Initial Price Offering is an offer to sell shares in a company to the investing public for the first time. The shares may be existing shares owned by the founders of the business who wish to realise profits from their investment, or new shares issued to raise additional capital for the company. Subsequent issues in the primary market include rights issue, stock split and scrip dividend.

Trading Activities
Equity Markets divisions of the major investment banks in London trade shares in two ways:

- Flow Trading – Buying and selling of lines of shares often in substantial amounts.
- Proprietary Trading – Traders hold shares i.e. take a position and seek to profit from short-term changes in the share price.

Market Size

Global issuance of equity and equity-related instruments totalled $505 billion in 2004, a 29.8% increase over the $389 billion raised in 2003. Initial public offerings by US issuers increased 221% with 233 offerings that raised $45 billion, and initial public offerings in Europe, the Middle East and Africa (EMEA) increased by 333%, from $9 billion to $39 billion.

The table below shows the volume of shares traded in the UK through the London Stock Exchange and the value over the last three years.

Table 2.5 Volume of shares traded on the London Stock Exchange

Year	Shares Traded	Value
2003	56.11 million	£4.1 trillion
2004	66.30 million	£4.7 trillion
2005	74.5 million trades	£4.8 trillion*

The value recorded was at November 2005
Source: London Stock Exchange, www.Londonstockexchange.com

Equity Derivatives

Equity derivatives are derivative instruments whose value is derived from the value of the underlying stock.

The following is a list of some of the equity derivative products on the market:

- Equity Call
- Equity Put
- Equity Swap
- Equity Index Derivative
- Variable Delivery Forward
- Barrier Options
- Equity Collar
- Monetising Equity Collar
- Protective Equity Put and Loan.

Indices

What are Indices?

Indices are statistical indicators providing a representation of the value of the securities which constitute them. Indices often serve as barometers for a given market or industry and benchmarks against which financial or economic performance is measured (www.investorwords.com).

Table 2.6 Common products across the asset classes

Product	Description	Uses	Balance sheet?	Credit risk	Where traded	Settlement/delivery	Amount	Date(s)
Foreign Exchange	Trading of one currency for another	Hedging/speculation in FX	Off balance sheet	Delivery risk; replacement risk	OTC	Usually full delivery	Any agreed amount	Spot or forward
Deposits	Borrowing/lending, usually interbank	Obtain/place funds unsecured, usually short term up to one year	On balance sheet	100% for depositor	OTC	Full delivery	Any agreed amount	Various periods. usually from spot
Certificates of deposit	Negotiable receipts for fixed periods	Investment/liquidity	On balance sheet	100% risk for the holder with the issuer	OTC	Full delivery of proceeds	Variable minimum. Usually any agreed amount	Usually fixed periods up to 5 years
FRAs	Forward/forward interest rate contract for a notional amount	Hedging/speculation in forward interest rate and arbitrage	Off balance sheet	Small/marginal (replacement)	OTC	Non-deliverable, cash settlement for interest rate differential on notional amount	Any agreed amount	Two (forward/forward) dates

Product	Description	Uses	Balance sheet?	Credit risk	Where traded	Settlement/delivery	Amount	Date(s)
Currency options	Contracts giving holder the the right to buy or sell FX at an agreed rate	Hedging/ speculation in interest rates	Off balance sheet	Marginal (replacement risk for holder buyer)	OTC and some central exchanges	OTC: usually full delivery on exercise/ value date; exchange traded are variable	Any agreed amount; exchange traded standardised	OTC: Euro- pean; fixed date; American period
Interest rate options	Contracts giving holder the right to buy or sell FX at agreed rate	Hedging/ speculation interest rates	Off balance sheet	Marginal/ replacement risk for option holder	OTC and some central exchanges	Usually cash management	Any agreed amount; OTC; exchange traded standardised	Agreed period
Interest rate swap	Agreements to swap interest rate commitments	Interest rate exposure management/ hedging arbitrage	Off balance sheet	Variable credit risk for both counterparties	OTC; recently exchanged traded	Cash settled; non-deliverable	Any agreed amount; OTC exchange traded standardised	Usually up to 10 years

Product	Description	Uses	Balance sheet?	Credit risk	Where traded	Settlement/delivery	Amount	Date(s)
Bonds	Negotiable borrowers certificate for term periods of over seven years	Investment, liquidity arbitrage	On balance sheet	Full credit risk for holders of proceeds	OTC	Full delivery	Any agreed amount	Fixed floating period, usually over 7 years
Repos	Purchase/resale agreements	Liquidity/ cashflow	On balance sheet	Very small	OTC	Full delivery	Any agreed amount	Usually short date
Financial structures	Financial transactions for set future date	Risk transfer/ hedge (speculation)	Off balance sheet	Virtually nil	Exchange traded	Generally cash settled, some deliverable	Standard/ fixed amount	Set periods long and short

FTSE

The FTSE 100 Index (pronounced footsie) is a share index of the 100 largest companies listed on the London Stock Exchange which meet a number of requirements set out by the FTSE Group. The requirements include having a full listing on the London Stock Exchange with a Sterling or Euro dominated price on SETS, and meeting certain tests on nationality, free float, and liquidity.

The index is seen as a barometer of success of the British economy and is the leading share index in Europe. It is maintained by the FTSE Group, a now independent company which originated as a joint venture between the Financial Times and the London Stock Exchange (hence the abbreviation Financial Times Stock Exchange). According to the FTSE Group's website, the FTSE 100 companies represent about 80% of the UK share market.

Major World Stock Market Indexes

- DAX 30 – Germany
- CAC 40 – France
- Euro Stoxx – European
- SMI – Switzerland
- MIB 30 – Italy
- IBEX35 – Spain
- Dow Jones – USA
- S&P 500 – USA
- Nasdaq 100 – USA
- Nikkei 225 – Japan
- Hang Seng – Hong Kong

MSCI Europe Index

The MSCI Europe Index is a free float-adjusted market capitalisation index that is designed to measure developed market equity performance in Europe. As of June 2006, the MSCI Europe Index consisted of the following 16 developed market country indices: Austria, Belgium, Denmark, Finland, France, Germany, Greece, Ireland, Italy, the Netherlands, Norway, Portugal, Spain, Sweden, Switzerland and the United Kingdom.

MSCI Emerging Markets Index

The MSCI Emerging Markets Index is a free float-adjusted market capitalisation index that is designed to measure equity market performance in the global emerging markets. As of June 2006, the MSCI Emerging Markets Index consisted of the following 25 emerging market country indices: Argentina, Brazil, Chile, China, Colombia, Czech Republic, Egypt, Hungary, India, Indonesia, Israel, Jordan, Korea, Malaysia, Mexico, Morocco, Pakistan, Peru, Philippines, Poland, Russia, South Africa, Taiwan, Thailand, and Turkey.

iTraxx

iTraxx is a family of Credit Default Swap indices products. The main index is the DJ iTraxx Investment Grade index covering 125 European credits. The index is rolled every six months based on a set of rules. The latest series is S4 which matures on December 20, 2010 for a 5Y contract. Other popular maturities include 7Y and 10Y.

Security Identifier Types

Security Identifiers should be mentioned in this section as they are used to identify either bonds or shares that are traded by the banks.

Definition
Security identifier types are the various methods by which a security product or issue is identified. They are each managed and distributed by different organisations.

Three different types that are commonly adopted in the UK will be discussed.

ISIN
An International Securities Identifying Number (ISIN) – pronounced icing – uniquely identifies a security. Its structure is defined in ISO 6166. Securities for which ISINs are issued include bonds, commercial paper, equities and warrants. The ISIN code is a 12-character alphanumerical code that does not contain information characterising financial instruments but serves for uniform identification of a security at trading and settlement.

ISINs are created only for securities and not derivatives such as options or futures. Additionally, securities offered on more than one stock exchange will use the same ISIN, which can make it problematic when trading in Europe where this is common.

CUSIP
The acronym CUSIP typically refers to both the Committee on Uniform Security Identification Procedures and the 9-digit alphanumeric security identifiers that they distribute for all North American securities for the purposes of facilitating clearing and settlement of trades. The CUSIP distribution system is owned by the American Bankers Association and is operated by Standard & Poor's. The CUSIP Services Bureau acts as the National Numbering Association (NNA) for North America, and the CUSIP serves as the National Securities Identification Number for products issued from both the United States and Canada.

RIC
A Reuters Instrument Code, or RIC, is a ticker-like code used by Reuters to identify financial-instrument types and indices. RIC codes use "artificial" tickers for common indexes and money market instruments. For instance, the US 10-year money market bond is assigned the ticker US10YT, the "T" at the end referring to "Treasury". Commodities are similarly assigned tickers, for instance crude oil is CL. Indexes have a leading period, for instance. DJI is the Dow Jones Industrial Average.

The Business Environment in Investment Banking

This chapter describes the business environment in which investment banks trade and encompasses the major players, the allied industries and regulators.

Introduction

The business environment in which investment banks operate is shaped by the following key economic factors:

- trade balance
- interest rates
- money supply
- exchange rate
- inflation
- government fiscal policy
- use of technology.

Trade Balance
The trade balance represents the difference between a country's exports and imports of goods and services. Importers are buyers and exporters are sellers of foreign currency. The excess of imports over exports will tend to bring downward pressure on the domestic currency. However, this effect is balanced by the fact that in modern global markets, currency flows are strongly influenced by international investment, both direct investment (buying foreign companies) and indirect investment (buying financial assets such as bonds and shares denominated in foreign currencies).

Impact: The trade balance will impact on the profitability of the banks in their respective base currencies and also present opportunities for speculative trading activities.

Interest Rates
Movements in interest rates can make a currency more attractive or unattractive to international investors. They could also impact on the cost of borrowing and lending.

Impact: Inter est rate movements will impact on the revenue generated from loans and deposits, other money market products, complex foreign exchange transactions and derivatives.

Inflation and Money Supply
Too much spending by a country's government can lead to excess growth in the money supply and inflation, which erodes the value of the currency.

Impact: Profits or losses will be made from speculative activities in the foreign exchange market.

Government Fiscal Policy
A government's fiscal stance will have a significant effect on the international standing of the local currency. If the government runs a budget deficit by spending more than it collects in tax revenues, the difference is made good by borrowing on the domestic or capital markets. Too much borrowing can lead to ris-

ing interest rates, which slows down economic growth and tends to adversely affect the market value of investment assets such as fixed income bonds and equities and makes the local currency less attractive as an investment vehicle.

Impact: Increased borrowing activity will increase the profits made from bonds, loans and deposits. However, profits or losses will be made from speculative activities in the foreign exchange market.

Exchange Rates

The movements in exchange rate of currency pairs are dependent mainly on interest rates and trade balance. Demand and supply of currencies dictate the exchange rate of one currency against the other. A currency will tend to become more valuable whenever demand for it is greater than the available supply. It will become less valuable whenever demand is less than the available supply (this does not mean people no longer want money, it just means they prefer holding their wealth in some other form, possibly another currency).

Impact: Fluctuations in exchange rates will have an impact on the profit or loss made by speculative trading by the dealers in the investment banks.

Stock Market

The stock market is the market for the trading of company stock, and a derivative of same. The global stock market is governed by the conventional market mechanism i.e. demand and supply.

There is also an event in the financial markets known as Initial Price Offering where common shares of a company are sold to public investors.

Impact: Investment banks generate revenue from underwriting these initial price offerings and also from the buying and selling of shares in the stock market.

Use of Technology

Technology has allowed the stock market to grow tremendously, and all the while society has encouraged the growth. Within seconds of an order for a stock, the transaction can now take place. Most of the recent advancements with trading have been due to the Internet. The Internet has allowed online trading. In contrast to the past where only those who could afford expensive stockbrokers could trade, anyone who wishes to be active in the stock market can now do so at a very low cost per transaction.

Impact: The investment banks now have a relatively cheap medium to execute stock trades. This will reduce transactions and increase profitability.

Players in Investment Banking

The business environment is made up of the following players:

- central banks
- the competitors (other banks and hedge funds)
- the exchanges – for example the London Stock Exchange and NASDAQ

■ allied organisations i.e. the regulators, credit agencies, new agencies, clearing houses
■ indices.

Exchanges and Government Central Banks

London Stock Exchange
The London Stock Exchange is a stock exchange located in London. Founded in 1801, it is one of the largest stock exchanges in the world, with many overseas listings as well as UK companies.

The LSE is broken down into the Main Market and Alternative Investments Market (AIM), as well as EDX London (which handles derivatives). The independent FTSE Group maintains a series of indices for measuring the LSE, including the FTSE 100 Index, FTSE 250 Index, and FTSE 350 Index.

European Central Bank
The European Central Bank (ECB) is in Frankfurt am Main. Germany is the central bank of the eurozone, in charge of monetary policy for the 12 countries that use the euro currency. The ECB's main task is to maintain the euro's purchasing power and thus price stability in the euro area. The ECB was established on June 1, 1998.

The central bank is the sole issuer of banknotes and bank reserves. That means it is the monopoly supplier of the monetary base. By virtue of this monopoly, it can set the conditions at which banks borrow from the central bank.

The Competitors
The UK investment banking sector consists mainly of banks whose headquarters are either in the US, Japan, Netherlands, France or Germany.

Overview of the Major Players in Investment Banking

Morgan Stanley
Morgan Stanley is a leading global financial services firm, offering a wide variety of products and services. Morgan Stanley comprises four main business units:

■ Institutional Securities
■ Individual Investor Group
■ Investment Management
■ Credit Services.

Some data on Morgan Stanley:

■ Founded: 1939
■ Revenue: $8.9 billion USD (Q2 200 6)
■ Employees: 53,163 (Aug 2006).

Goldman Sachs

Goldman Sachs, Inc. is one of the world's oldest and most prestigious invest-ment banks and is known simply as "The Firm" in some financial circles. Gold-man Sachs is divided into three major segments:

- Investment Banking
- Trading and Principal Investments
- Asset Management and Securities Services.

Some data on Goldman Sachs:

- Founded: 1869
- Revenue: $10.10 billion USD (Q2 2006)
- Employees: 22,425 (2005).

Merrill Lynch

Merrill Lynch & Co. Inc., usually referred to as Merrill Lynch, is an investment banking and stock brokerage company. As one of the world's largest financial management and advisory companies, it has one of the more recognisable names in the world of finance.

Some data on Merrill Lynch:

- Founded: 1914
- Revenue: $8.2 billion USD (Q2 2006)
- Employees: 56,000 (2006).

JP Morgan Chase

JP Morgan Chase & Co., a financial holding company, was formed in 2000 with the merger of the Chase Manhattan Corporation and J.P. Morgan & Co.
Some data on JP Morgan Chase:

- Revenue: $14.94 billion USD (Q2 2006)
- Employees: 168,461 (as of June 30, 2005).

Investment Bank Ranking

Investment banks are ranked according to the dollar volumes of the deals they work on, usually exhibited in league tables. League tables are used in two con-texts: either in promotional materials or client pitches produced by an invest-ment bank, or tabulated by a financial information tool, such as Thomson Finan-cial or Bloomberg.

Growing concerns about credibility of league tables have led some banks to use actual screenshots of Bloomberg's league tables in their materials to emphasise that no tweaks were used to manipulate the ranking. The selection bias of only showing the favourable rankings still holds however. In order to get the most complete information, one should access leagues tables on Bloomberg, Thomson Financial, or any other reputable source (they all rely on a third-party database that actually stores information on all announced deals).

Table 3.1 is an example of a league table based on Market size.

Table 3.1 Equity Underwriters Leaders 1 January 2004 – December 31 2004 (based on $ value) by Market Size

	#1 Ranked bookrunner	Proceeds ($ millions)	Market Share(%)	Number of Shares	Market Size ($ millions)	Market Issues
Stocks and Bonds						
Global debt, Equity & Equity-related:						
	Citigroup	534,486.2	9.4	1,892	5,693,011.6	20,066
Global Disclosed Fees:						
	Citigroup	1,717.4	11.1	724	15,400.6	6,890
Stocks						
Global Equity & Equity-related:						
	Morgan Stanley	54,268.7	10.7	184	505,098.9	3,628
Global Convertible Offerings:						
	Morgan Stanley	10,483.1	10.7	46	98,436.4	469
Bonds						
All International Bonds:						
	Citigroup	202,957.9	8.3	531	2,433,995.2	5,068
All International Bonds in Euros:						
	Deutsche	80,355.5	7.8	303	1,025,579.6	2,529
Loans						
Global Loans:						
	JP Morgan	499,900.5	18.9	1,153	2,639,843.7	7,147
European Leveraged Loans:						
	Royal Bank of Scotland	16,006.6	13.6	64	117,337.1	233

Source: Thomson Financial

Allied Organisations

Allied organisations to the investment banking industry include the regulators, the news agencies, the clearing houses and credit rating agencies. The following are some of the allied organisations that service the UK investment banking industry.

The Regulators

Financial Services Authority

The Financial Services Authority (FSA) is an independent non-departmental public body and quasi-judicial body that regulates the financial services industry in the United Kingdom. Its main office is based in Canary Wharf, London, with another office in Edinburgh. When acting as the competent authority for listing of shares on a stock exchange, it is referred to as the UK Listing Authority (UKLA) and maintains the Official List.

The FSA's main role in the investment banking community is to regulate the banks as well as reduce financial crime. Investment banks have to comply with sets of regulations that govern the financial industry and have a requirement to report their activities to the FSA.

Bank for International Settlements

The Bank for International Settlements (or BIS) is an international organisation of central banks which exists to "foster cooperation among central banks and other agencies in pursuit of monetary and financial stability". The BIS also provides banking services, but only to central banks or to international organisations like itself.

The BIS based in Basle, Switzerland, was established in 1930 and is the world's oldest international financial organisation.

ECNs

An Electronic Communication Network (ECN) is a computer system that facilitates trading of financial products outside stock exchanges. The primary products that are traded on ECNs are stocks and currencies.

In order to trade with an ECN, one must be a subscriber. ECN subscribers can enter limit orders into the ECN, usually via a custom computer terminal or a direct dial-up. The ECN will post those orders on the system for other subscribers to view. The ECN will then match contra-side orders (i.e. a sell-order is "contra-side" to a buy-order with the same price and share count) for execution. Generally, the buyer and seller are anonymous, with the trade execution reports listing the ECN as the party.

Some ECNs may offer additional features to subscribers such as negotiation or reserve size, and may have access to the entire ECN book (as opposed to the "top of the book") that contains important real-time market data regarding depth of trading interest.

There are five main FX ECNs in the UK as follows:

- Fxall – founded by HSBC, Goldman Sachs, Morgan Stanley, Credit Suisse, Bank of America, JP Morgan Chase and UBS.
- Currenex – an independent venture backed by Barclays Capital amongst others.
- FX Connect – owned by State Street.
- Hotspot FXi – privately owned by independent venture capitalists.
- 360T – owned by independent private investors funded by venture capitalists.

The following banks are members of the above-named ECNs:

Table 3.2 Investment Bank Membership of UK-based ECNs

Bank	Fxall	Currenex	FXConnect	HotspotFXi	360T
ABN AMRO	Y	Y	Y	Y	Y
Bank of America	Y		Y		Y
Bank of New York	Y				
Barclays Capital	Y	Y	Y	Y	Y
Bear Stearns	Y	Y	Y	Y	
Credit Suisse	Y		Y		
Deutsche Bank	Y	Y	Y		
Goldman Sachs	Y		Y		
Lehman Brothers	Y	Y	Y		Y
Merrill Lynch	Y	Y	Y		
Morgan Stanley	Y		Y		
Rabobank		Y	Y		Y
WestLB			Y	Y	

Source: LondonFX
Key: Y indicates membership
*Some of the banks listed above may be members but may not be fully connected as yet.

The Credit Rating Agencies

A credit rating agency (CRA) is a company that assigns credit ratings for issuers of certain types of debt obligations. In most cases, these issuers are companies, cities, non-profit organisations, or national governments issuing debt-like securities that can be traded on a secondary market. A credit rating measures credit worthiness, the ability to pay back a loan, and affects the interest rate applied to loans. Interest rates are not the same for everyone, but instead are based on risk-based pricing, a form of price discrimination based on the different expected costs of different borrowers, as set out in their credit rating. There exist more than 100 rating agencies worldwide.

Uses of Credit Rating Agencies
Credit ratings are used by investors, issuers, investment banks, broker-dealers, and by governments. For investors, credit rating agencies increase the range of investment alternatives and provide independent, easy-to-use measurements of relative credit risk; this generally increases the efficiency of the market, lowering costs for both borrowers and lenders. This in turn increases the total supply of risk capital in the economy, leading to stronger growth.

Table 3.3 Investment grade credit ratings

Rating (s)	Description
Aaa	Obligations rated Aaa are judged to be of the highest quality, with minimal credit risk.
Aa1, Aa2, Aa3	Obligations rated Aa are judged to be of high quality and are subject to very low credit risk.
A1, A2, A3	Obligations rated A are considered upper-medium grade and are subject to low credit risk.
Baa1, Baa2, Baa3	Obligations rated Baa are subject to moderate credit risk. They are considered medium-grade and as such may possess certain speculative characteristics.

Moody's

Moody's Corporation is the holding company for Moody's Investors Service, which performs financial research and analysis on commercial and government entities. The company also ranks the credit-worthiness of borrowers using a standardised ratings scale. The company has a 40% share in the world credit rating market.

Moody's Ratings

Long-term Obligation Ratings – Moody's long-term obligation ratings are opinions of the relative credit risk of fixed-income obligations with an original maturity of one year or more. They address the possibility that a financial obligation will not be honoured as promised. Such ratings reflect both the likelihood of default and any financial loss suffered in the event of default.

Special

D (in default), WR (withdrawn rating), NR (not rated), (P) (Provisional).

Short-term Ratings

Moody's short-term ratings are opinions of the ability of issuers to honour short-term financial obligations. Ratings may be assigned to issuers, short-term programmes or to individual short-term debt instruments. Such obligations generally have an original maturity not exceeding 13 months, unless explicitly noted.

Moody's employs the following designations to indicate the relative repayment ability of rated issuers:

Standard and Poor's

Standard & Poor's (S&P) is a subsidiary of McGraw-Hill that publishes financial research and analysis on stocks and bonds. It is one of the top three players in this business, along with Moody's and Fitch Ratings. It is well known for its US-based S&P 500 and the Australian S&P 200 stock market index.

Table 3.4 Speculative grade credit ratings

Rating (s)	Description
Ba1, Ba2, Ba3	Obligations rated Ba are judged to have speculative elements and are subject to substantial credit risk
B1, B2, B3	Obligations rated B are considered speculative and are subject to high credit risk.
Caa1, Caa2, Caa3	Obligations rated Caa are judged to be of poor standing and are subject to very high credit risk
Ca	Obligations rated Ca are highly speculative and are likely in, or very near, default, with some prospect of recovery of principal and interest
C	Obligations rated C are the lowest rated class of bonds and are typically in default, with little prospect for recovery of principal or interest

Table 3.5 Speculative grade credit ratings

Rating (s)	Description
Ba1, Ba2, Ba3	Obligations rated Ba are judged to have speculative elements and are subject to substantial credit risk
B1, B2, B3	Obligations rated B are considered speculative and are subject to high credit risk.
Caa1, Caa2, Caa3	Obligations rated Caa are judged to be of poor standing and are subject to very high credit risk
Ca	Obligations rated Ca are highly speculative and are likely in, or very near, default, with some prospect of recovery of principal and interest
C	Obligations rated C are the lowest rated class of bonds and are typically in default, with little prospect for recovery of principal or interest

Long-term Credit Ratings
Investment Grade

Table 3.6 Investment grade credit ratings

Rating (s)	Description
AAA	The best quality companies, reliable and stable
AA	Quality companies, a bit higher risk than AAA
A	Economic situation can affect finance
BBB	Medium-class companies, which are satisfactory at the moment

Non-Investment Grade (also known as junk bonds)

Table 3.7 Non-Investment Grade credit ratings

Rating (s)	Description
BB B	More prone to changes in the economy Financial situation varies noticeably
CCC	Currently vulnerable and dependent on favourable economic conditions to meet its commitments
CC	Highly vulnerable, very speculative bonds
C	Highly vulnerable, perhaps in bankruptcy or in arrears but still continuing to pay out on obligations
CI	Past due on interest
R	Under regulatory supervision due to its financial situation
SD	Has selectively defaulted on some obligations
D	Has defaulted on obligations and S&P believes that it will generally default on most or all obligations
NR	Not rated

Credit ratings

As a credit rating agency, Standard & Poor's issues credit ratings for the debt of companies. As such, it is designated a Nationally Recognised Statistical Rating Organisation by the US Securities and Exchange Commission.

It issues both short-term and long-term credit ratings. See Tales 3.6 and 3.7.

News Agencies and Market Data Providers

What are News Agencies?

A news agency is an organisation of journalists established to supply news reports to organisations in the news trade: newspapers, magazines, and radio and television broadcasters. They are also known as wire services or news services.

News agencies can be corporations that sell news, cooperatives composed of newspapers that share their articles with each other, or commercial newswire services which charge organisations to distribute their news. Governments may also control "news agencies", particularly in authoritarian states like China and the Soviet Union. A recent rise in Internet-based alternative news agencies, as a component of the larger alternative media, have emphasised a "non-corporate view" as being largely independent of the pressures of business media.

News agencies generally prepare hard news stories and feature articles that can be used by other news organisations with little or no modification, and then sell them to other news organisations. They provide these articles in bulk electronically through wire services (originally they used telegraphy; today they frequently use the Internet). Corporations, individuals, analysts and intelligence agencies may also subscribe. The business proposition of news agencies might thus be responsible for the current trends in separation of fact-based reporting from Op-eds.*

The following are notable news agencies and market data providers that service the investment banking industry.

Reuters

Reuters Group plc is best known as a news service that provides reports from around the world to newspapers and broadcasters. However, news reporting accounts for less than 10% of the company's income. Its main focus is on supplying the financial markets with information and trading products. These include market data, such as share prices and currency rates, research and analytics, as well as trading systems that allow dealers to buy and sell such things as currencies and shares on a computer screen instead of by telephone or on a trading floor like that of the New York Stock Exchange.

Some 330,000 financial market professionals working in the equities, fixed income, foreign exchange, money, commodities and energy markets around the world use Reuters' products. They rely on Reuters' services to provide them with the information and tools they need to help them be more productive.

Bloomberg

Bloomberg L.P. is a financial news service founded by Michael Bloomberg in 1981. It provides real-time and archived financial and market data, pricing, trading, news and communications tools in a single, integrated package to corporations, news organisations, financial and legal professionals and individuals around the world using the Bloomberg terminal and Bloomberg media services.

Bloomberg has grown to include a global news service, including television, radio, the Internet and publications. The financial newswire service, Bloomberg News, comprises 1,600 reporters in 94 bureaux worldwide, writing more than 4,000 news stories daily.

Thomson Financial

Thomson Financial is an arm of The Thomson Corporation, one of the world's leading information companies, focused on providing integrated information solutions to business and professional customers.

Thomson Financial has many offices across the US, Europe, and Asia Pacific regions. The company has a wide variety of financial products which grows and changes rapidly according to market need. *Thomson ONE* is a core product,

---

* Op-eds are pieces of writing expressing an opinion.

although legacy branded offerings such as *Datastream Advance* and *Global Topic* will probably remain for a few years.

Thomson ONE is a competitor of Bloomberg and Reuters. It is currently known as one of "The Big Three".

CQG

CQG, a real-time, graphic-enhanced quotation vendor, inserts all exchange corrections in real time. According to the company's website, http://www.cqg.com:

> "It was established in 1980 to supply data and market analyses to futures traders. The company has pioneered many new technologies in offering professional traders real-time and historical financial information integrated into an extensive graphic and technical analysis application, and many of its innovations have become industry standards.
>
> "Three separate networks ensure uninterrupted data transmission, and CQG's Data Quality Group monitors a worldwide data network 24 hours a day to ensure that customers get the clean data they need, when they need it. CQG is the only vendor that inserts all exchange corrections in real time to provide accurate, integrated information to traders."

The Financial Times

The Financial Times (FT) is an international business newspaper printed on distinctive salmon pink broadsheet paper. The periodical is printed in 22 cities: London, Leeds, Dublin, Paris, Frankfurt, Stockholm, Milan, Madrid, New York, Chicago, LA, San Francisco, Dallas, Atlanta, Miami, Washington DC, Tokyo, Hong Kong, Singapore, Seoul, Dubai and Johannesburg.

The *FT* reports extensively on business and features extensive share and financial product listings. It also has a sizeable network of international reporters – 400 journalists in 50 editorial bureaux worldwide – covering current affairs in general. *The Financial Times* is normally seen as centre-right/liberal, although to the left of its principal competitor, *The Wall Street Journal*. It advocates free markets and is generally in favour of globalisation.

Morgan Stanley Capital International (MSCI)

Morgan Stanley International Inc. is a global provider of equity (US and International) fixed income and hedge fund indices. MSCI provides global equity indices, which, over the last 30+ years, have become the most widely used international equity benchmarks by institutional investors. MSCI constructs global equity benchmark indices that contribute to the investment process by serving as relevant and accurate performance benchmarks and effective research tools, and as the basis for various investment vehicles.

Close to 2,000 organisations worldwide currently use the MSCI international equity benchmarks. MSCI estimates that over USD 3 trillion are currently benchmarked to these indices on a worldwide basis.

MSCI also provides a wide range of fixed income indices for the investment community, including indices for Sovereign, Investment Grade and High Yield debt markets, as well as the Interest Rate Swaps market.

FISD

The Financial Information Services Division (FISD) of the Software & Information Industry Association (SIIA) provides a forum for exchanges, market data vendors, specialist data providers, brokerage firms and banks on distribution, management, administration and use of market data. The FISD was founded in 1985 and is governed by a 27-member Executive Committee of exchanges, vendors and market data user firms.

The following investment banks are members of FISD:

- ABN AMRO
- Bank of America
- Bear Stearns
- Credit Suisse
- Goldman Sachs
- Morgan Stanley
- UBS.

Clearing Houses

What is a Clearing House?

A clearing house is an independent organisation, appointed by an exchange, which guarantees securities transactions. It completes the transactions on that exchange by seeing to validation, delivery, and settlement. A clearing house may also offer novation, the substitution of a new contract or debt for an old, or other credit enhancement services to its members.

London Clearing House

The organisation, founded in 1888 to clear sugar and coffee trades in London, was originally known as the London Produce Clearing House. Once LCH has registered a trade, it becomes the buyer to every LCH Member who sells and seller to every LCH Member who buys, thereby guaranteeing that the financial obligations of trades are met.

The LCH clears trades conducted on the International Petroleum Exchange (IPE), the London International Financial Futures Exchange (LIFFE) incorporating the London Commodity Exchange (LCE), the London Stock Exchange and the London Metal Exchange (LME). It is owned by the major UK clearing banks (Barclays, Lloyds TSB, HSBC, Royal Bank of Scotland and Standard Chartered) and is a recognised Clearing House under the regulatory supervision of the Financial Services Authority (FSA).

The London Clearing House Limited and Clearnet S.A. merged in 2004 to form the LCH.Clearnet Group. LCH.Clearnet will help achieve a widely sought-after goal – the consolidation of European Central Counterparty infrastructure, helping transform the efficiency and effectiveness of the EU's capital markets.

Settlement Banks

What is a Settlement Bank?

A settlement bank is a bank that provides settlement services to investment banks for their transactions.

Euroclear

Euroclear is the world's premier settlement system for domestic and international securities transactions, covering bonds, equities and investment funds.

Market owned and market governed, Euroclear provides securities services to major financial institutions located in more than 80 countries. In addition to its role as the leading International Central Securities Depositary (ICSD), Euroclear also acts as the Central Securities Depository (CSD) for Dutch, French, Irish and UK securities.

The Euroclear system clears a wide range of international fixed and floating rate paper, as well as domestic debt instruments. Participants are able to confirm, clear and settle in many currencies, on a delivery versus payment basis.

Euroclear owns the Crest settlement system, which along with settlement of fixed income instruments and funds provides a range of asset servicing and asset optimisation services, including full corporate actions facilities.

Clearstream

Clearstream Banking S.A. (CB) is the clearing division of Deutsche Börse, based in Luxembourg. It was created in January 2000 through the merger of Cedel International and Deutsche Börse Clearing, part of the Deutsche Börse Group, which owns the Frankfurt Stock Exchange. Cedel, established in 1971, specialised in clearing and settlement. In 1996 it obtained a bank licence. In July 2002, Deutsche Börse purchased the remaining 50% of Clearstream International for €1.6 billion. Deutsche Börse's strategy is to be a vertical securities silo, providing facilities for the front and back ends of securities trading. By 2004 Clearstream contributed €114 million to Deutsche Börse's total Earnings Before Interest and Taxes (EBIT) of €452.6 million. It handled 50.0 million transactions and was custodian of securities worth €7,593 trillion.

The purpose of Clearstream is to facilitate money movements around the world, particularly by handling the resolution of sales of European stocks and bonds, in which market Clearstream was a major player, with an estimated 40% market share until May 2004 – together with its competitor Euroclear, the two firms settle 70% of European transactions.

Trends in Investment Banking

4

This chapter covers the trends that are shaping the investment banking industry from the regulations introduced by regulators to the product ranges that are creating markets for the banks.

Introduction

There are various regulations and technological advances that are constantly creating changes in the investment banking sector. The banks invest a vast amount of money in compliance and systems upgrade projects which provide employment to the relevantly skilled professionals. Below are a few of the regulations and technologies that govern trends in investment banking.

Sarbanes Oxley Act of 2002

The Sarbanes-Oxley Act of 2002 is a United States federal law, also known as the Public Company Accounting Reform and Investor Protection Act of 2002 (and commonly called SOX or SarbOx).

The Act covers issues such as establishing a public company accounting oversight board, auditor independence, corporate responsibility and enhanced financial disclosure. It was designed to review the dated legislative audit requirements and is considered one of the most significant changes to the United States' securities laws since the New Deal in the 1930s. The Act gives additional powers and responsibilities to the US Securities and Exchange Commission.

The Act came in the wake of a series of corporate financial scandals, including those affecting Enron, Tyco International, and WorldCom (now MCI). It was named after sponsors Senator Paul Sarbanes and Representative Michael G. Oxley.

SOX requires public companies with market capitalisation of $75 million, listed on US exchanges, to have IT controls in place. IT controls are specific information systems designed to allow support, oversight and monitoring of business processes. IT controls generally include controls over the general IT environment, computer operations, access to programs and data, program development and program changes.

The American investment banks have ongoing SOX programmes and IT staff are involved in the testing of IT controls being developed.

Basel 2 Accord

Basel 2 is shorthand for the "New Basel Capital Accord". The original Basel Accord was agreed in 1988 by the Basel Committee on Banking Supervision. The 1988 Accord, now referred to as Basel 1, helped to strengthen the soundness and stability of the international banking system. Basel 2 is a revision of the existing framework, which aims to make the framework more risk sensitive and representative of modern banks' risk management practices.

This revised capital adequacy framework will further reduce the probability of consumer loss or market disruption as a result of prudential failure. It will do so by seeking to ensure that the financial resources held by a firm are commensurate with the risks associated with the business profile and the control environment within the firm. The new Basel Accord will be implemented in the Europe Union via the Capital Requirements Directive (CRD).

The new framework requires that the following types of risk are incorporated into banks' decision-making processes:

- Credit Risk – The possibility that a bond issuer will default by failing to repay principal and interest in a timely manner.
- Operational Risk – The risk associated with the potential for systems, i.e. people, technology and processes, failure in a given market.
- Market Risk – The risk which is common to an entire class of assets or liabilities i.e. the economic changes that impact on a market as a whole.

Basel 2 consists of three "pillars" as follows:

- Pillar 1 of the new standards sets out the minimum capital requirements firms will be required to meet for credit, market and operational risk.
- Pillar 2 requires firms and supervisors to take a view on whether a firm should hold additional capital against risks not covered in Pillar 1 and take action accordingly.
- Pillar 3 aims to improve market discipline by requiring firms to publish certain details of their risks, capital and risk management.

There are quite a number of Basel 2 projects in the major investment banks. There are systems being developed to allow for the reporting of capital adequacy and computation of the Risk Weighted Assets/Capital Requirements from the following parameters:

- PD (Probability of Default) – which measures the likelihood that the borrower will default over a given time horizon.
- LGD (Loss Given Default) – which measures the proportion of the exposure that will be lost if a default occurs.
- EAD (Exposure at Default) – which for loan commitments measures the amount of the facility that is likely to be drawn if a default occurs.
- Maturity – which measures the remaining economic maturity at exposure.

The Future

Work is apparently already underway on Basel 3, at least in a preliminary sense. The goals of this project are to refine the definition of bank capital, quantify further classes of risk and further improve the sensitivity of the risk measures.

AML/ KYC

AML stands for "Anti Money Laundering" while KYC stands for "Know Your Customer". The laundering of money or assets to camouflage criminal activities such as global terrorism, drug trafficking or illegal tax evasion is well known,

41

given the high-profile political measures taken to prevent these activities. According to the International Monetary Fund (IMF), money laundering accounts for between two and five per cent of the world's GDP, with the most conservative estimates from international law enforcement agencies being in excess of a $300 billion annual ballpark figure globally.

Investment banks have to proactively manage risks associated with the menace of money laundering. These risks are illustrated in Figure 4.1.

Investment banks have to comply with a Financial Action Task Force (FATF) directive, which requires due diligence and maintenance of attribute records of the following:

- counterparty IDs
- registered name and address
- country of registration
- business purpose
- parent and trading relationships
- information on regulator
- exchange listing
- list of directors
- lists of shareholders for the business entity.

Figure 4.1 Risks associated with AML/KYC

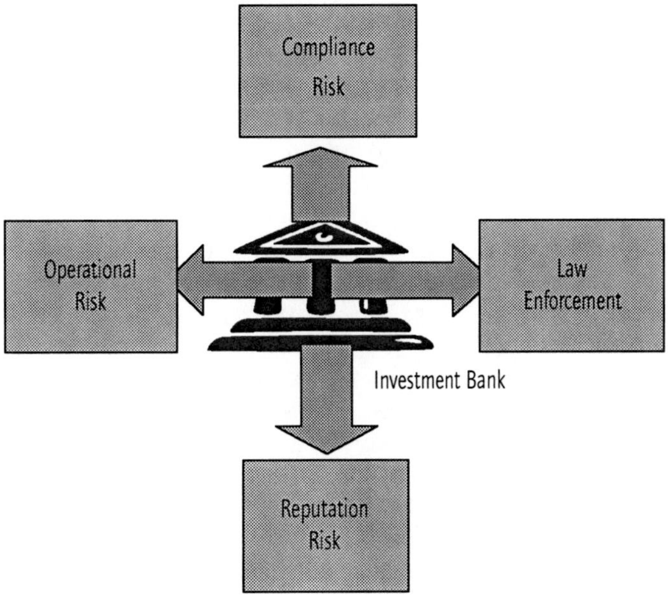

There are other AML guidelines for banks to follow:

■ JMLSG guidelines
  ▓ enhanced KYC procedures;
  ▓ patterns of normal transactions to create profiles and monitoring;
  ▓ abnormal transactions/activity;
  ▓ risk-based approach for capturing additional information.
■ Global AML principles for Correspondent Banking (Nov. 2002)
  ▓ risk indicators like Correspondent Banking client's domicile, ownership & management structures, business and customer base;
  ▓ updating the client's risk profile on a risk-assessed basis.

There are IT projects in a number of the investment banks for AML/KYC compliance.

Straight-through Processing

Straight-through processing (STP) enables the entire trade process for capital markets and payments transactions to be conducted electronically without the need for rekeying or manual intervention, subject to legal and regulatory restrictions. The concept has also been transferred into other asset classes including energy (oil, gas) trading.

Presently, the entire trade lifecycle, from initiation to settlement, is a complex labyrinth of manual processes taking several days. STP is at least "same day" or faster, ideally minutes or even seconds. The goal to minimise settlement risk is for the execution of a trade and its settlement and clearing to occur simultaneously. However, for this to be achieved, multiple market participants must realise high levels of STP. In particular, transaction data would need to be made available on a just-in-time basis, which is a considerably harder goal to achieve for the financial services community than the application of STP alone. After all, STP itself is merely an efficient utilisation of computer-based technology in transaction processing.

Historically, STP solutions were needed to help financial markets firms meet the move to one-day trade settlement of equities transactions, as well as to meet the global demand that had resulted from the explosive growth of online trading. Now the concepts of STP are applied to reduce systemic and operational risk, improve certainty of settlement and minimise operational costs.

When fully realised, STP will provide asset managers, brokers/dealers, custodians and other financial services players with tremendous benefits, including greatly shortened processing cycles, reduced settlement risk and lower operating costs. Some industry analysts believe that STP is not an achievable goal in the sense that firms are unlikely to find the cost/benefit to reach 100% automation. Instead they promote the idea of improving levels of internal STP within a firm while encouraging groups of firms to work together to improve the quality of the automation of transaction information between them, either bilaterally or as a community of users (external STP). However, in some systems the concepts of STP have been refined to straight-through exception processing (SteP), whereby steps and filters automate the back-office workflow.

43

Continuous Linked Settlement (CLS)

CLS is a financial clearing system established in 1997 to enable banks to settle foreign exchange transactions on a "Payment versus Payment" basis, also known as PVP. When a foreign exchange trade is settled, each of the two parties to the trade pays out (sells) one currency and receives (buys) a different currency; PVP ensures that these payments and receipts happen simultaneously. Without PVP there is a (small) chance that one party could pay out without receiving; this is known as settlement risk or Herstatt risk.

CLS was created by many of the world's largest banks and began operation in September 2002. Technically it is a bank regulated by the Federal Reserve Board of New York. Since it began operation, it has rapidly become the standard method of foreign exchange settlement between major banks and as of December 2005 it settles about 100,000 trades a day with a value of about US$2 trillion.

The following investments banks are some of the shareholders of CLS:

- Bank of America
- Bank of New York
- Barclays bank
- BNP Paribas
- Credit Lyonnais
- Credit Suisse
- Deutsche Bank (including the shareholders of former Bankers Trust).

The following currencies are the 15 currencies that are settled by CLS:

- Australian Dollar
- Canadian Dollar
- Danish Krone
- Euro
- GB Pound
- Hong Kong Dollar
- Japanese Yen
- Korean Won
- New Zealand Dollar
- Norwegian Krone
- Singapore Dollar
- South African Rand
- Swedish Krona
- Swiss Franc
- US Dollar.

Growth of Credit Derivatives Market

Introduction
The development of credit derivatives is a logical extension of two of the most significant developments of the present time: securitisation and derivatives. The concept of a derivative is to create a contract that derives from an original contract or asset. For example, stock market derivatives are contracts that are settled based on movements in the prices of stocks, without transferring the underlying stock. Similarly, a credit derivative involves a contract between parties in relation to the returns from a credit asset, without transferring the asset as such.

The securitisation process has become increasingly popular over the last decade, with structures ranging from the simple passing on of cash flows from underlying assets, to complex structures utilising credit derivatives.

Definition of Credit Derivatives
Credit derivatives can be defined as arrangements that allow one party (protection buyer or originator) to transfer the credit risk of a reference asset, which it may or may not own, to one or more other parties (the protection sellers).

Types of Credit Derivatives
The easiest and the most traditional form of a credit derivative is a guarantee. Financial guarantees have existed for thousands of years. However, the present-day concept of credit derivatives has travelled much farther than a simple bank guarantee. The credit derivatives currently being used in the market can be broadly classified into the following:

- Credit Default Swaps
- Credit Linked Notes
- Collaterised Debt Obligations.

Market Size
According to Celent, a research and consulting firm:

> "The credit derivatives market has developed at a breathtaking rate. In the early 1990s, the market was virtually nonexistent; by 2002 it was valued at slightly over US$2 trillion notional outstanding and Celent expects it to exceed US$7 trillion by 2006. And new types of credit derivative products have been introduced at a dizzying pace.
>
> Credit derivatives still account for just slightly more than one per cent of the overall market for derivative contracts among commercial banks. However, the overall derivatives market increased less than three-fold from 1997 to 2003, while the credit derivatives market grew nearly sixteen times over."

A report by the British Banking Association (BBA) also estimated the global market in Credit Derivatives would rise to $8.2 trillion by the end of 2006 and

45

Figure 4.2 Global Notional Outstanding in Credit Derivatives Market

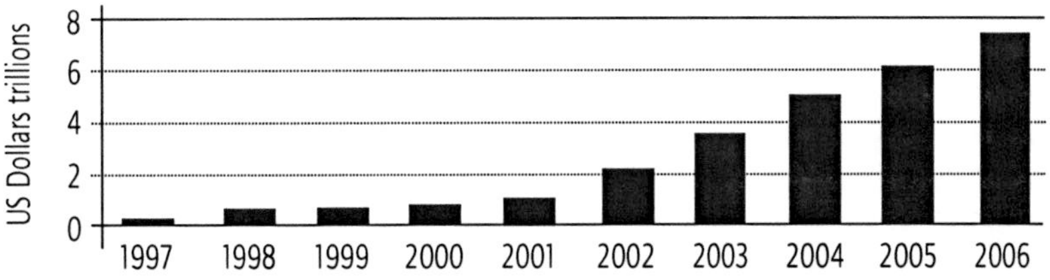

London is expected to maintain pole position as the global leader with over 66% of all trades booked in the world occurring in London.

Given the rapid growth of the credit derivatives market, there will be a number of IT projects in the various banks as they adapt their trading systems to accommodate trading of these instruments.

Growth of New Hedge Funds

Definition of a Hedge Fund

First of all, what are hedge funds? The following are two definitions of hedge funds:

- "A multitude of skill-based investment strategies with a broad range of risk and return objectives. A common element is the use of investment and risk management skills to seek positive returns regardless of market direction." (Goldman Sachs)
- A private, unregistered investment pool vehicle for directional investing by using techniques like selling assets short or long.

Hedge Fund Market

Over the last decade, the growth of hedge funds accelerated dramatically, in terms of both assets under management and number of funds. Although precise figures are difficult to obtain, recent industry reports estimate that there are now between 4000 and 6000 hedge funds worldwide, managing a total wealth of $400–600 billion (see Figure 4.3). This is compared to a figure of about 600 hedge funds worldwide in 1990, with less than $200 billion of assets; and the implied growth rate of 25% should continue to apply in the future according to KPMG and RR Capital Management Corp.

Characteristics of "New" Hedge Funds
- Hedge funds' managers are partners, not employees.
- Hedge funds have limited transparency.
- Hedge funds strategies are not scalable.
- Hedge funds target specific investors.

Hedge Funds Investment Styles

The most common types of investment styles for Hedge Funds are:

- equity hedge/long/short funds
- relative value/market neutral
- global macro
- event driven
- convertible arbitrage
- short selling
- emerging markets
- distressed securities.

Figure 4.3 Assets managed by the hedge fund industry: assets are expressed in billions of dollars

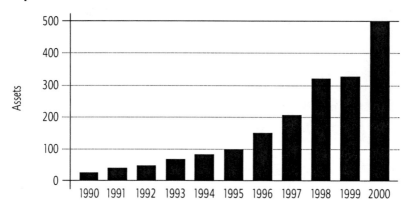

©Hedge funds - Myths and Limits, Francois Serge L'Habitant. 2003. Copyright John Wiley & Sons Limited. Reproduced with permission.

Categories of Hedge Fund Investor

Table 4.1 Assets managed by the hedge fund industry: assets are expressed in billions of dollars

Type of Investor	Investable assets
Ultra-high net worth individuals	More than $50 million
High net worth individuals	$5–50 million
Affluent investor	$1–5 million

Structure of a typical Hedge Fund

The typical "new hedge fund" is made up of the following departments:

- portfolio management
- research department
- operations
- trading
- risk management

Growth of the Prime Brokerage Function

Prime Brokerage is a service sold by investment banks to hedge funds. The following "core services" are typically bundled into the Prime Brokerage package:

- global custody (including clearing, custody, and asset servicing);
- securities lending;
- financing (to facilitate leverage of client assets);
- customised technology (provide hedge fund managers with portfolio reporting needed to effectively manage money);
- operational support (prime brokers act as a hedge fund's primary operations' contact with all other broker dealers).

In addition, certain prime brokers provide additional " value-added" services, which may include some or all of the following:

- capital introduction
- office space leasing and servicing
- risk management advisory services
- consulting services.

As hedge funds have proliferated globally through the 1990s and 2000s, prime brokerage has become an increasingly competitive field and an important contributor to the overall profitability of the investment banking business. Morgan Stanley and Goldman Sachs in their individual annual reports attributed revenue of over $1 billion in 2004 to prime brokerage operations.

The following investment banks are known to be providing prime brokerage services at present:

- JPMorganChase
- Bank of America
- Barclays Capital
- Bear Stearns
- Citigroup
- Credit Suisse
- Deutsche Bank

- Dresdner Kleinwort Wasserstein
- Goldman Sachs
- Lehman Brothers
- Merlin Securities
- Merrill Lynch
- Morgan Stanley
- Pershing LLC, a subsidiary of Bank of New York
- UBS.

Internet as a Medium for the Hedge Fund Business

The development of the Internet has attracted the attention of asset managers as a convenient, efficient and economical means of marketing, selling and providing information on products and service to a global audience. The high accessibility and low cost have created a tendency to use this new media in a more informal way to conduct securities-related business.

Growth of the Internet Investment Banks

Internet Investment Banks are making inroads into the traditional investment banking market, especially in the area of underwriting. The door to Internet underwriting has already been opened by online brokers, who offer customers IPO shares through partnerships with traditional city-based investment banks, but new Net investment banks want to go further.

These Internet banks aim to woo issuing companies with cheaper prices, the same idea behind the ultra-successful online brokers. They use Internet road shows, electronic trading and electronic information distribution to bring big savings over traditional methods.

But many observers believe that to compete for significant underwriting jobs, online investment banks will have to borrow just as much from the traditional investment banks as from the Internet revolution, which could undercut their advantages.

These online banks also provide services such as Foreign Exchange (FX), Contract for Difference stock derivatives (CFDs) and equities trading. Notable examples of Internet investment banks include Saxo bank, a Danish bank and Synthesis bank, a Swiss investment bank.

Growth of Emerging Markets Derivatives

Local derivatives markets in emerging markets have grown rapidly over the past few years, especially in countries that have removed capital controls and developed their underlying securities markets. The growing use of derivative products by emerging markets' participants has also supported capital inflows and helped investors to price and manage the risks associated with investing in emerging markets more efficiently.

Despite this rapid growth, emerging markets derivatives account for only one per cent of the total outstanding notional in global derivatives markets. Local derivatives markets in emerging economies differ greatly in their sizes, both in absolute terms and relative to cash markets. Compared with mature markets, the ratio of outstanding notional value of derivatives to market capitalisation of the underlying asset markets is fairly small in most emerging economies. The most common problems that constrain the development of local derivatives are as follows:

- relatively underdeveloped markets for underlying instruments;
- weak/inadequate legal and market infrastructure;
- restriction on the use of derivatives by local and foreign entities.

Types of Derivatives traded in Emerging Markets

Currency Derivatives
Most of the currency derivatives trading around the world takes place in the over-the-counter (OTC) markets, with foreign exchange swaps accounting for two-thirds of the turnover. In emerging markets, the most liquid OTC currency derivatives markets are in Singapore, Hong Kong SAR, and South Africa.

By contrast with Singapore, Hong Kong SAR and South Africa, a significant share of currency derivatives trading in Brazil takes place at an organised exchange – Bolsa de Mercadoris & Futuros of Sao Paolo (BM&F).

Fixed Income Derivatives
In contrast to recent trends in global currency derivatives markets, the global fixed income derivatives market continued to expand steadily over the past few years, with interest rate swaps (IRS) being the largest and the fastest growing market segment. In emerging market countries, the most liquid fixed income derivatives markets are in Singapore, Hong Kong SAR, Brazil, Mexico and South Africa (see Table 4.2). In Latin America and Singapore, most of the fixed income derivatives trading takes place at the organised exchanges; in both Korea and South Africa it is mainly concentrated in the OTC market (see Table 4.2).

Equity Derivatives
Compared to currency and fixed income derivatives, equity-based derivatives products represent a much smaller part of the global market, with the bulk of activity concentrated at the organised exchanges. While most exchanges in emerging Asia experienced steady expansion in equity derivatives products over recent years, the stock index derivatives' growth in Korea was spectacular. As a result, Korea now accounts for about 30 per cent of global turnover in stock index derivatives. Outside Asia, South Africa has the most developed equity derivatives market in the emerging markets universe. Equity derivatives products are traded on the Johannesburg Stock Exchange (JSE) and the South African Futures Exchange (SAFEX).

Table 4.2 Exchange Traded Options and Futures Contract Trading Volume 2002

	Stock	Equity Index	Govt Debt	Interest Rate	Foreign Exchange
Latin America					
Brazil	89,740,296	6,979,515	15,320	51,116,740	18,179,225
Mexico	–	49,243	3,579,165	80,606,463	52,180
Asia					
Singapore	13,690	10,458,364	699,448	21,714,364	–
Hong Kong SAR	3,745,816	6,995,635	3,673	281,227	–
Korea	57,918	1,933,072,470	12,802,781	3,788	1,436,191
Taiwan Province of China	–	7,944,254	–	–	–
Malaysia	–	233,864	80,419	64,307	–
EMEA					
South Africa	10.326,227	19,018,736	32,765	–	–
Hungary	365,150	282,973	–	–	–
Poland	92,097	3,322,855	–	–	5,957

Source: International Federation of Stock Exchange

© Mathieson Donald et al, International Monetary Fund 2004. Reproduced with permission.

Credit Derivatives

The emerging credit derivatives market mainly consists of credit protection instruments on external sovereign bonds that are traded offshore. The share of emerging market instruments in global credit derivatives is much larger than their share in other global derivatives markets. The most commonly used credit derivatives in emerging markets are credit default swaps (CDSs), credit-linked notes (CLNs), and collateralised debt obligations (CDOs).The sovereign CDSs are the most liquid instruments in the emerging credit derivatives market, accounting for around 85 per cent of the total outstanding notional. The most actively traded contracts reference external sovereign bonds issued by Korea.

Deutsche Bank establishes a ranking of countries according to liquidity levels based on the frequency of trades in the default swap market, as shown in Table 4.3.

Trading in Weather Derivatives

Weather derivatives are financial instruments that can be used by organisations or individuals as part of a risk management strategy to reduce risk associated

Table 4.3 Liquidity Levels

Most Liquid	Less Liquid	Sporadic Activity
Argentina	Bulgaria	Chile
Brazil	Croatia	Ecuador
Mexico	Peru	Ivory Coast
Russia	Korea	Morroco
Turkey	Thailand	Kazakhstan
Columbia	–	Lithuania
Venezuela	–	Tunisia
South Africa	–	Romania
Phillippines	–	

Source: IMF

with adverse or unexpected weather conditions. Weather derivatives ensure that corporates are in a position to meet investor expectations and deliver profits by meeting their cash flows even in the face of bad weather. The difference to other derivatives is that the underlying asset (rain/temperature/snow) has no direct value to price the weather derivative. Farmers can use weather derivatives to hedge against poor harvests caused by drought or frost, theme parks may want to insure against rainy weekends during peak summer seasons and power companies may use heating degree days (HDD) contracts to smooth earnings.

Weather derivatives contracts initially began trading over the counter in 1997. As the market for these products grew, the Chicago Mercantile Exchange introduced the first exchange-traded weather futures contracts (and corresponding options) in 1999. The CME currently trades weather derivative contracts for 18 US cities, nine European cities and two cities in Japan.

Why Trade in Weather Derivatives?

Weather derivatives are different from weather insurance covers. In the latter case, a claim is paid on account of adverse weather, which needs to be proved, while in the derivative version, the payment is made the moment weather turns against you.

Weather derivatives are a cheaper alternative to insurance and can tide over the cyclical weather-related risks. The cost of a weather derivative depends upon the probability of adverse impact on account of the weather, and the duration of the contract signed between the bank and the corporate entity.

Market Size

The weather derivatives market is estimated at $12 billion by Pricewaterhouse Coopers. The notional value of weather risk management contracts transacted from April 2004 through March 2005 nearly doubled from $4.3 billion in the 2004 annual survey to $8.4 billion, according to its 2005 annual industry survey, representing an 83 per cent increase over the previous year and an all-time high for the industry.

In the energy and agriculture sectors, there has been tremendous growth in the trading of weather risk contracts. The investment community has also helped drive major growth in the over-the-counter (OTC) market, where notional value has increased 50% from $2.8 billion to $4.2 billion. Increased participation was seen in 2005 from financial institutions such as banks and hedge funds, which see weather derivatives as a vibrant new marketplace in which to operate, in addition to specialist weather dealers and (re)insurers.

Market Players

The organisations in the weather derivatives market include:

- energy marketers/utilities
- insurance/reinsurance
- transformers
- financial institutions
- OTC Derivatives
- insurance.

The major player in the industry is RaboBank, with a significant share of the market, and it has experienced growth rates of 500 per cent in the current year. Other players include banks such as ABN Amro and Credit Lyonnais.

Who uses Weather Futures?

Current users of weather futures are primarily energy companies in energy-related businesses. However, there is growing awareness and signs of potential growth in the trading of weather futures among agricultural firms, restaurants and companies involved in tourism and travel. Many OTC weather derivative traders also trade CME weather futures for the purpose of hedging their over-the-counter transactions.

Introduction of Markets in Financial Instruments Directive (MiFID)

What is MiFID?

MiFID is a directive that will replace the existing Investment Services Directive (ISD), the most significant European Union legislation for investment intermediaries and financial markets since 1995. MiFID extends the coverage of the current ISD regime and introduces new and more extensive requirements to which firms will have to adapt, in particular in relation to their conduct of business and internal organisation.

According to IBM consulting, "Fundamental, far-reaching and disruptive are three words to describe MiFID. When it comes into force in November 2007, it will impose a comprehensive regulatory regime on investment service firms and markets throughout the European Union."

MiFID is of increasing concern in the investment banking community from a project management perspective. Investment banks are now realising the potential impact of the directive and time is running out; planning for MiFID is complex and onerous.

According to the FSA website www.fsa.gov.uk:

"MiFID is a major part of the European Union's Financial Services Action Plan (FSAP), which is designed to create a single market in financial services. MiFID comprises two levels of European legislation. 'Level 1', the Directive itself, was adopted in April 2004. In several places, however, it makes provision for its requirements to be supplemented by 'technical implementing measures', so-called 'Level 2' legislation.

MiFID has the same basic purpose. But it makes significant changes to the regulatory framework to reflect developments in financial services and markets since the ISD was implemented.

Most firms that fall within the scope of MiFID will also have to comply with the new Capital Requirements Directive (CRD), which will set requirements for the regulatory capital which a firm must hold. Those firms newly covered by MiFID will be subject to directive-based capital requirements for the first time."

Impact on Firms

In general MiFID will cover most if not all firms currently subject to the ISD, plus some that currently are not. This will include:

- investment banks
- portfolio managers
- stockbrokers and broker dealers
- corporate finance firms
- many futures and options firms
- some commodities firms.

Key Provisions

Scope

New developments include bringing investment advice within the scope of EU regulation. Commodity derivatives are now a financial instrument for the purposes of MiFID but not all firms trading commodity derivatives are within the scope of the directive. This will depend on whether they fall within an exemption contained in MiFID:

- organisational requirements
- passporting rights
- client classifications

■ regulated market and MTF standard
■ pre-trade equity transparency
■ transaction reporting.

More information about MiFID can be found on the FSA website.

Implications for IT Professionals

MiFID will create opportunities in investment banks in Europe for IT professionals in the following areas:

■ Project Management – managing the IT projects across business divisions and coordinating efforts from staff in legal, compliance, operations and IT.
■ Impact Analysis – analysis of how MiFID will impact on business divisions, operational functions and IT systems and gaps in compliance.
■ Interaction with other ongoing projects – MiFID implementation will interact with other ongoing projects such as AML/KYC compliance.
■ Implementation of systems solutions – systems solutions have to be delivered for implementation of MiFID for areas such as best execution, compliance monitoring, data storage and retrieval and trading systems enhancement.

Some notable application vendors such as GL Trade and IBM have solutions that the investment banks could deploy to comply with MiFID.

Introduction of IAS39

International Accounting Standard 39: Financial Instruments: Recognition and Measurement (IAS 39) is one of the accounting standards that must be complied with for companies reporting under International Financial Reporting Standards (IFRS). It defines the valuation and reporting of financial instruments, such as derivatives, loans and employee option schemes.

Basically, IAS 39 requires changes to the value of financial assets to have a profit and loss effect, and it defines valuation techniques. Financial instruments used for hedging, as strictly defined in the standard, are exempt from a P&L effect under normal circumstances. IAS 39 is a long and controversial standard which attempts to regulate in detail an area of innovation in corporate finance, so interpretation and application of the standard will prove difficult. IAS 39 is heavily influenced by the work of United States' accounting standards setters. IAS 39 also advances the accounting profession's attack on historical value as the basis for balance sheet valuation.

Popularity of Financial Spread Betting

Spread Betting is a tool that enables traders to profit from both up and down moves on a wide variety of financial markets, whether stock indexes, individual

55

shares, currencies, bonds, and commodities such as gold or crude oil. What differentiates spread betting from other types of financial speculation is that all profits are 100% tax free.

Spread Betting Markets

The following are financial-based markets that traders bet on:

- stock indexes
- currencies
- commodities
- sector bets
- bonds
- grey markets.

Use of Financial Spread Bets

- For speculation in any financial, commodity or currency market worldwide, within the one account.
- Hedging of risks.

Popularity of Contracts for Difference (CFDs)

What are CFDs?

A contract for difference, also commonly known as a CFD, is an equity derivative that allows users to speculate on share price movements, without the need for ownership of the underlying shares. CFDs are traded over the counter (OTC).

Contracts for differences allow investors to take long or short positions and unlike futures contracts, they have no fixed expiry date or contract size. Trades are conducted on a margined basis with margins typically starting at ten per cent for CFDs on leading equities.

CFDs are currently available in listed and/or over-the-counter markets in the United Kingdom, Germany, Switzerland, Italy, Singapore and Australia. Some other securities markets have plans to issue CFDs in the near future, such as Hong Kong. CFDs have varying brand names depending on who issues them. For example, they are sometimes called Turbo Certificates or Waves. In Hong Kong they are referred to as Callable Bull/Bear Contracts (CBBCs). Contracts for differences are not permitted in the United States, due to restrictions by the US Securities and Exchange Commission on OTC financial instruments.

They have now become widespread, with some commentators suggesting that up to 25 per cent of UK stock market turnover is attributable to CFDs.

Players in the CFD markets include:

- Barclays dealers
- City Index
- CMC markets

▓ GCI Trading
▓ GNI Touch.

Growth of Syndicated Lending

What is syndicated lending?

A syndicated loan is a loan or credit granted to a borrower by a syndicate formed by a group of banks or other financial institutions (approved to conduct credit business) under the same loan terms and agreements.

Syndicated loans involve many banks; each member bank holds different titles: lead bank, arranging bank, underwriting bank, allied bank, high-level managerial bank, managerial bank or participating bank. Syndicated loans include three types of member banks from a functional perspective:

▓ Lead Bank: at customer's trust, plan and organise syndicate, arrange banks to underwrite the loan. Lead Bank only guarantees the underwriting of the loan amount they commit. Lead Bank can be one bank or joined by many banks.
▓ Participating Bank: at the invitation of lead bank to participate in loan syndicate, and provide loan according to the amount agreed.
▓ Correspondent Bank: responsible for lending and management after legal documents signed.

The Correspondent Bank is usually the Lead Bank or its subsidiaries, but also can be determined through discussion between member banks.

The syndicated loans market is a global market. Most of the loans granted are used to finance projects on an international basis, i.e. the funds may come from participating banks anywhere in the world to fund a project in another country.

Growth of the Syndicated Loan Market

The syndicated loan market is a major part of the operations of banks throughout the world, with major centres in London, New York and Hong Kong. They are typically used to finance big projects, for example: the $11 billion Citigroup lent Koch Industries to help finance its proposed $13.2 billion acquisition of Georgia-Pacific Corp. in the US. According to the *Financial Times*, the financing is believed to be one of the largest loans on record by a single bank.

Figure 4.4 shows the amount of syndicated loans arranged globally in the years 1992–2003. It shows that total amounts raised annually have more than tripled during this period, despite the fact that the number of individual loans has slipped back over the last three years.

According to Thomson Financial, in the first nine months of 2005, global syndicated loan volume surged 28.3 per cent to $2.3 trillion, compared with $1.9 trillion in the prior year period. In the third quarter alone, global syndicated lending volume totalled $722.1 billion, up from $626.1 billion in the third quarter of 2004.

Figure 4.4 Global Syndicated Loan Borrowing from 1992 to 2003

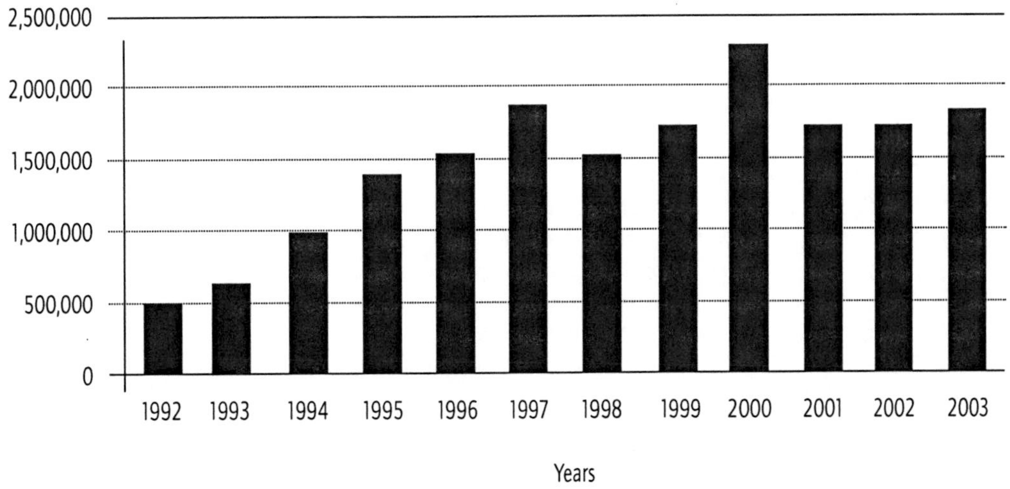

Source: Syndicated Lending

Major Players in the Market
Table 4.4 shows the major players in the market.

Table 4.4 Largest syndicated loans lenders in the US in 2004

Name	Market Share
JP Morgan	32.1%
Bank Of America	20.4%
Citigroup	15.3%
Wachovia	6.0%
Deutsche Bank	3.4%
Credit Suisse	3.2%
Barclays	1.8%
Lehman Brothers	1.7%
Goldman Sachs	1.0%
UBS	1.0%

Source: Thomson Financial League table

Adoption of FpML

FpML (Financial products Markup Language) is an XML message standard for the OTC Derivatives industry. All categories of privately negotiated derivatives will eventually be included within the standard. The standard is managed by ISDA* on behalf of a community of investment banks that make a market in OTC derivatives.

As of March 2006, FpML 4.1 is the latest (recommendation) version. The core scope includes the products of Foreign Exchange (FX) Swaps and Options, Interest Rate Swaps, Swaptions, Credit Default Swaps, Credit Default Swap Indices, Equity Options, Equity Swaps, Total Return Swaps and many others. The core processes include trading, valuation, confirmation, novations (also known as assignments), increases, amendments, and terminations.

The FpML community is currently working on version 4.2, which already includes additional product support for Inflation Swaps, Asset Swaps, Credit Default Swap Baskets, and Tranches on Credit Default Swap Indices. New processes included are allocations, position reporting, cash flow matching, as well as a formal definition of party roles.

Participants

The following investments banks are major participants in the definition of FpML:

- Bank Of America
- Barclays Capital
- BNP Paribas
- Credit Suisse
- Deutsche Bank
- Goldman Sachs
- JP Morgan Chase
- Morgan Stanley
- RBS
- UBS.

59

* ISDA stands for International Swaps for Derivatives Association.

Overview of the Generic Trading Lifecycle

*This chapter gives a brief description of the phases
of the trading lifecycle as it pertains to any product
in the financial markets, regardless of the asset class.*

Introduction

All trades – whether foreign exchange, money markets, loan or deposit, derivative transaction or repo – have certain common characteristics. All require entry into the bank's system to be recorded for verification, confirmation, settlement and reconciliation. This process ensures transactions are properly recorded and enables correct accounting in the books of a bank and accurate risk management measurement.

Definition of Trading Lifecycle

The trading lifecycle can be defined as a sequence of events that pass through the front, middle and back office.

The stages of the trading lifecycle are follows:

- trade capture
- verification and confirmations
- settlement
- netting
- reconciliations
- accounting.

Figure 5.1 gives a diagrammatic representation of the generic trading lifecycle and associated processes.

Trade Capture

Trade capture for all transaction types is usually on a screen-based system, and can be through manual input or feed from another live trading system. The following are some of the activities that are carried out during the trade capture process:

- Front-office employees evaluate a trade's potential, the associated market risk and counterparty risk to assess the "fit" of the trade.
- Front-office applications are usually integrated to limits' checking systems to ensure that the credit limit for the counterparty involved in the trade has not been exceeded.
- Limits are checked for the trader and the counterparty ensuring that the credit limit for the counterparty involved in the trade has not been exceeded.
- Static data and live streaming market data are fed into the trading system.
- Market data is used to construct curves for pricing instruments that are to be traded.
- Typical data input into the system include instrument name, values, counterparty name, book/account name; data input requirements vary for each trade capture system or trade type.

61

- Traders consider the value added to their open positions held, and the likely profit and loss impact.
- Middle-office staff, the risk managers, evaluate the effects of the aggregate trades booked within the firm's portfolios and the global positions held. VaR (value-at-risk), Monte Carlo simulations and other statistical tools are used to perform these evaluations.
- Data is validated on entry against defined criteria and exceptions, such as calculations of a value of an FX deal not agreeing with the exchange rate, or interest calculation not agreeing with interest rate. These are reported on the screen, with the transaction unable to progress until the problem is resolved.

Investment banks are increasingly standardising on the use of standard settlement instructions (SSIs) as advised by the regulatory authorities as an important factor in reducing errors and streamlining the settlement process. SSIs are almost invariably used where they are in place. To assist in reconciliation procedures, some banks have separate agents for FX, money market and derivatives.

Reports are generated intraday and at the end of day for the trading activities. In some cases, trades are uploaded to the trade capture system by traders to offset positions on their books.

Verification and Confirmation

The next step in the trading lifecycle is verification and confirmation and some of the activities involved are as follows:

- Once the trade has passed validation the checking can begin.
- In trade capture systems, the essential elements of the trade are matched (verified) when the deal is done.
- Trades that have the settlement date the same as the trade date, like some spot foreign exchange deals, require telephone confirmations as an extra security check.
- The relevant category of SWIFT messages is exchanged with counterparties in the trade to confirm details of the trade.
- There are different categories of SWIFT messages for the different trade types, i.e. FX, money market or derivatives.
- The essential generic information included in a confirmation for all deals consists of: reference number, type of transaction, name and location of counterparty, price dealt, amount(s) and currency(ies) involved, and details of the transaction, including action and value dates and settlement instructions.

Figure 5.1 The Generic Trade Lifecycle

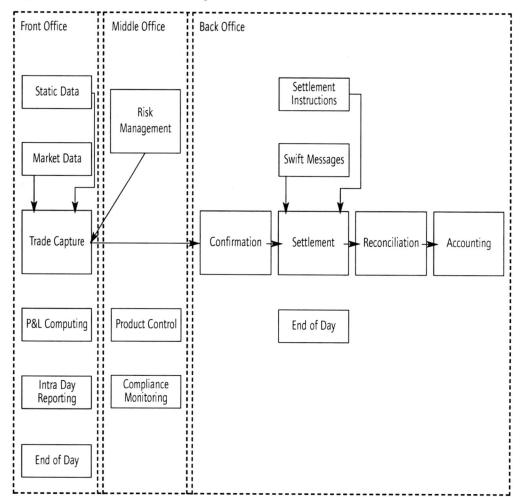

Settlement and Netting

Settlement and netting is the next phase of the trading lifecycle and some of the activities involved are as follows:

- Once confirmation has been completed, a trade is ready for settlement. Depending on the transaction, this can take many forms. It can range from settlement of an FX trade on the value date, or cash settlement of difference for many derivatives, through to delivery against payments for bonds or securities.
- The back-office operations staff process the trade. The principal concern is that the settlement of the trade is completed.

63

Table 5.1 Examples of SWIFT messages

Type	Description
MT 100	Customer Transfer
MT 103	Single Customer Credit Transfer
MT 200	Financial institution transfer for its own account
MT 210	Notice to receive
MT 300	Foreign Exchange Confirmation
MT 396	CLS Status Advice
MT 502	Order to buy or sell via a third party
MT 900	Confirmation of Debit
MT 940	Customer Statement Message
MT 942	Interim Transaction Message
MT 950	Statement Message

All SWIFT messages include the literal "MT" (message type). This is followed by a three-digit number that denotes the message type, category, and group.

▓ Most products have several events during their life. For example, a loan may be paid away at the start date, have interim payments, reprice interest if on a floating-rate basis and finally be repaid with interest at maturity.

▓ Bank treasury systems have been developed to produce the required SWIFT message to meet the event on the required date using the MT 200 series via their gateway into the SWIFT system. This message will be generated to, say, a correspondent agent bank or national payments carrier.

▓ A final check of payments is carried out before releasing their payments file to ensure everything is correct.

▓ If a netting agreement is in place, then netting is performed.

Reconciliation

Cash reconciliation falls into two categories: internal (positions) and external (Nostro accounts representing agents' correspondents' accounts).

What is Nostro?

Nostro is a banking term to describe an account that a bank holds with a foreign bank. Nostro accounts are usually in the currency of the foreign country.

A Nostro account is a demand deposit account or a current account, deposited by a local bank with the foreign bank in the currency of the country where the money is held. Mostly, both banks usually have business relations or are counter parties or are correspondent banks. It is also called "Correspondent account" or "Our account".

The purpose of Nostro reconciliation is to agree the cash entries that have been passed over the bank's internal Nostro accounts, representing transactions that are starting or maturing on a given value date, with the actual cash movements at the bank's agent account. Thus expected cash movements are compared with actual cash movements.

Reconciliations are based on exception reporting. Typically, an incoming SWIFT file will be matched to an outstanding deals file using a proprietary software package or an in-house developed tool. Matched, probable match or unmatched reports are produced, based on key fields such as value date, value, counterparty etc.

Accounting

Accounting is usually considered to be the last phase of the trading lifecycle and some of the activities involved in the accounting process are as shown below:

- Accounting entries are usually generated based on a code profile held for product type on a time event basis.
- Transactions in base or counter currencies are tracked and revalued. This is for the purpose of determining profit and loss.
- Forward books of outstanding items in the portfolio will normally be revalued on a marked-to-marked basis.

Post-Trade Operations

The following are common post-trade operations that take place in investment banking:

- amendment
- cancellation
- cancellation and reissue
- early take-up
- close out
- allocation.

Trading in Foreign Exchange

This chapter covers the analysis of the FX trading lifecycle based on an FX spot transaction between two fictitious investment banks, Big Bank Trust and US Street, and the discussion of pricing elements of FX trading.

Introduction

As seen in the last chapter there are a set of activities involved in the trading lifecycle of any asset class. Also in Chapter 2 we briefly discussed the foreign exchange market. In this chapter we will discuss the market further and analyse the trading lifecycle of foreign exchange using a case study for FX spot trading.

What is an FX Spot Trade?
An FX spot trade is a transaction whereby one currency is exchanged for another for immediate delivery, which usually means two business days, i.e. the value date, after the deal is agreed.

The main medium that facilitates the transfer of funds is the SWIFT system, through the exchange of different categories of messages between counterparties and their correspondent banks.

Definition of Value Dates
Value dates are the dates on which FX trades settle, i.e. the date that the payments of each currency are made. The value dates for most FX trades are referred to in the market as "spot", and as stated is two business days from the trade date, denoted as (T+2). The most notable exception to this rule is USD/ CAD, which has a spot date one business day from the trade date, denoted as (T+1). Spot dates for CAD crosses (e.g. GBP/CAD) normally take the spot date of the crossed currency pair and are therefore T+2.

Buying and Selling Currencies

As stated in Chapter 2, it should be noted that currencies are always priced in pairs. When traders wish to execute a trade on the FX market, they expect the currency they receive to increase in value relative to the one they give up. In order to realise a profit, they must reverse the original exchange when the currency received increases in value otherwise they will have an open position. An open position is the results of any trade or trades executed, without including any profits or losses realised.

FX Spot Quotation
In an FX spot quotation for a given currency pair (e.g. EUR/USD), the first currency in the pair is considered as the base currency while the second currency is known as the counter or quote currency. In most cases the US dollar is the base currency but there are exceptions, i.e. when the quotes are against pounds sterling, the euro and the Australian dollar. In these cases the US dollar is quoted as the counter currency.

FX spot prices are usually quoted to between four and six significant figures. For example, EUR/USD, the most frequently traded currency pair, has seen rates such as 0.8225, 1.0015 or 1.2928. The number of decimals does not vary for a particular currency pair according to movements in the rate, except in the case of devaluations.

FX spot prices have a bid price and an offer price, for example:

	Bid	Offer
EUR/USD	1.0342	1.0344

The convention for the quotation for EUR/USD in pips is 1.0342/44. Pips is an acronym for "Percentage in Points" and it is the fourth decimal place, which is 1/100th of 1%.

For illustration, EUR is denoted as CCY1 and USD as CCY2. The bid price is where the bank is willing to buy CCY1 and the offer price is where the bank is willing to sell CCY1. In this case, the bank is willing to buy EUR against USD at 1.0342 and is willing to sell EUR against USD at 1.0344. The difference between the bid and the offer is called the spread; the above example is a 2 pip spread. It is market convention always to talk about what you are doing with CCY1. For example, if someone is "buying USD/JPY", they are buying USD and selling JPY.

Market participants are generally expected to know what the first part of the rate will be (in this case 1.0342), and this part is known as the "big figure". Because the current big figure does not usually vary from one minute to the next, traders normally quote only the last two digits of the rate (three digits for some currency pairs), and these digits are known as the "pips". A trader would therefore quote the bid and offer in this example as "42 44". When trading over the phone, it is common to quote only the pips, whereas e-commerce systems generally display the entire rate, although the pips may be given more prominence.

EUR/GBP is displayed in a slightly different way from most other currency pairs in that although one pip is worth 0.0001, the rate is often displayed to five decimal places. The fifth decimal place can only be 0 or 5 and is used to display half pips. Many trading systems display the half pip digit in a smaller font than the two main pip digits.

Interbank trades are always traded in CCY1 amounts, regardless of the currency pair. Most customer trades are also traded in CCY1 amounts, although many customers have a business need to trade in CCY2 amounts. For example, even though EUR/USD is a standard currency pair, a US customer may have a need to trade a USD amount rather than a EUR amount. The rate is quoted in exactly the same way, but instead of multiplying the EUR amount by the EUR/USD rate to product a USD amount, the USD amount is divided by the EUR/USD rate to produce a EUR amount.

Market Terminology

Typical interbank traded amounts in major currency pairs such as EUR/USD include amounts such as USD 5 million and USD 10 million, and amounts are usually quoted in millions. A billion (1,000,000,000) is called a "yard", which originates from the French "milliard". For example, traders say "ten dollars" to mean USD 10,000,000, say "half a quid" to mean GBP 500,000 and say "three yards of Yen" to mean JPY 3,000,000,000.

The market has its own verbal abbreviated names for major currencies. For example, USD/CAD is known as "Dollar Canada", USD/JPY is known as "Dollar Yen", and AUD/USD is known as "Aussie Dollar". An exception is GBP/USD, which is known as "Cable", which stems from the days when a cable under the Atlantic Ocean was used to synchronise the GBP/USD rate between the London market and the New York market.

Decimal places on spot rates

The following rules can be used to determine how many decimal places a spot rate should have:

- Spot rates should have four or five significant figures and an even number of decimal places.
- Digits for fractional pips (e.g. the fifth decimal on EUR/GBP) are in addition to, and not included within, an even number of decimal places.
- Six significant figures may used in some rare cases, for example if the rate is between 10 and 100 (e.g. USD/MXN[1], USD/ILS[2]) or between 1000 and 10000 (e.g. USD/KRW[3]), but still with an even number of decimal places.

Cross-Currency Rates

A cross-currency rate is an FX rate between two currencies that is determined by using their exchange rate against a common currency, usually the US dollar. An example is shown below for determining the cross rate between GBP and CHF.

The GBP/CHF cross rate will be determined from two standard interbank currency pairs; EUR/GBP and EUR/CHF. The following is the quote for these rates:

	Bid	Offer
EUR/GBP	0.6640	0.6644
EUR/CHF	1.5745	1.5748

In order to calculate the cross rate from the bid and offer rates, the bid is divided by offer and then offer is divided by the bid.

Therefore:

GBP/CHF bid = 1.5745/ 0.6645 = 2.3695

GBP/CHF offer = 1.5748/0.6642 = 2.3708

---

1 MXN = Mexican New Peso
2 ILS = Israeli Shekel
3 KRW = Korean Won

69

Note that the cross rate is calculated via EUR rather than USD because EUR-based currency pairs are more liquid for most European currencies than USD-based currency pairs.

Lifecycle of an FX deal

In order to analyse the FX trading lifecycle, an FX spot trade between Big Bank Trust and US Street will be used as a case study. Shown below is a diagrammatic representation of the FX trading lifecycle.

Figure 6.1 The FX Trading Lifecycle

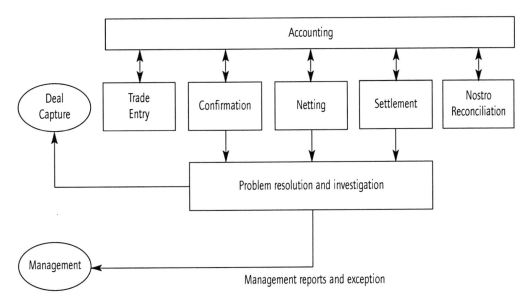

Amos, G and Nolan, D Mastering Treasury Office Operations.

Scenario of the FX Spot Trade

FX dealers in investment banks that wish to trade currencies would quote rates at which they intend to carry out the transaction via telephone, "squarkbox", web-based systems or the Reuters network.

On January 10 2007, a spot FX trader at Big Bank Trust, an investment bank in London, quotes the spot FX rate on the Reuters network: GBP: USD 1.6559/69. Note here that the bid rate = 1.6559 and the offer rate = 1.6569.

The trader agrees a deal with a counterpart at US Street bank, an investment bank in New York.

Big Bank Trust, London, sells 1,000,000 GBP against USD to US Street bank, New York. The exchange rate is 1.6569.

On January 12 2007, Big Bank will transfer the sterling to the Nostro account US Street bank has with TBD bank in London. US Street bank, in turn, transfers US dollars to Big Bank's Nostro account with BOC bank in New York.

Note here that the trade date is 10 January, 2007 and the value date is 12 January 2007.

Trade Capture

Trade capture for an FX spot transaction takes place on a screen-based trading system. The following are the activities that are carried out in the trade capture phase:

■ Pre-trade limits' checking is carried out to ensure that the limits for the trader and/or the counterparty are not exceeded if the trade is undertaken.
■ The following data items are usually manually entered in screen-based trading systems for the FX Spot trade:

Table 6.1 Data items for FX Spot trade

Field	Description
Direction	Denotes whether currency CCY1 is bought or sold
CCY 1	The entered currency of the trade
CCY 2	The calculated currency of the trade
CCY1 amount	The entered amount of the trade
CCY2 amount	The calculated amount of the trade = CCY1 amount * spot trade
Spot rate	Exchange rate between CCY1 and CCY2
Value date	Date at which the trade will be settled. Always equal to the spot date for the CCY pair
Counterparty	Identifier for the customer with whom the trade is transacted
Portfolio	Portfolio whose position will be impacted by the trade

■ For this scenario the following fields will be populated on the deal entry screen with the values shown:

Table 6.2 Data values

Field name	Value	System Populated?
Counterparty	US Street	N
Book name	BigBook	N
Trade Reference Number	Bg123ocp	Y
Portfolio name	BigPort	N
Direction	Sell	Y
Trade Date	10-Jan-2007	Y
Settlement date	12-Jan 2007	N
Value date	12-Jan 2007	Depends on system
CCY1	GBP	N
CCY2	USD	N
Amount CCY1	1,000,000	N
Amount CCY1	1,656,900	N
Pricing Environment	Europe USD Curve	Y (from market data feed)

■ Depending on the system, some of the fields on the trade capture screen are manually populated whilst others are populated by the system.
■ Market data such as exchange rate is fed into the live trading environment to complete the trading data required.
■ SSIs (Standard Settlement Instructions) are exchanged between counterparties via SWIFT message MT293.
■ When the trade capture details have been completed, the trade is submitted.
■ The trade is now entered into the relevant book.
■ Depending on the system, the trade details are either manually or system verified.

Confirmation
■ For FX spot trades, MT300 SWIFT messages are exchanged by the counterparties as confirmation of the trade.
■ Typical data contained in the MT300 messages include the following:
  ■ sender
  ■ receiver
  ■ general information
  ■ sender's reference
  ■ type of operation
  ■ common reference
  ■ transaction details

* trade date
* value date
* exchange rate
* currency, amount bought
* receiving agent
* currency amount sold
* receiving agent
* dealing method.

The confirmation messages are matched to ensure that the essential elements of the trade correspond.

Netting

Once confirmation has been completed, netting is the next step. Netting is essentially a mutual obligation that is settled at a net value of a contract as opposed to its gross dollar value.

There two types of netting payment arrangements in the FX markets, namely bilateral and multilateral netting.

What is Multilateral Netting?

Multilateral Netting is a process by which companies within a corporate group can make substantial savings on foreign exchange payments and receipts.

This is achieved by summing and converting each participant's inter-company and (optionally) third-party payments and receipts into a single local-currency amount.

Before implementing a netting system each company may have several payments to make to the other companies in the group. Each payment may cover many invoices. They will have to make the payments and then inform all the receivers of the specific invoices that are covered by the payment, which in turn need to be reconciled.

With a netting agreement in place, instead of making the payments directly, each company sends the payment information (or invoices themselves) to the Netting Centre.

The Netting Centre calculates each subsidiary's net position in its home currency and makes the payment to the company or, in the case of a receipt, instructs the company to send the payment to the Netting Centre.

One of the obvious benefits of netting is that transaction costs are reduced because fewer payments are made.

What is Bilateral Netting?

Bilateral netting is when two counterparties agree to net foreign exchange payments and receipts to one another. They sign a master agreement specifying the types of netting to be performed.

There are clearing houses that provide FX netting services covering the main financial centres. Notable amongst them is Exchange Clearing House Organisation (ECHO).

The netting process would typically include a service by SWIFTNet Accord which enables real-time matching and exception handling for the FX spot trade. The service basically involves matching the MT300 messages sent by the counterparties to the trade. Depending on the outcome of the reports that are output from the matching process, the bilateral netting process can proceed. The Accord reports are sent as an MT398 if any of the counterparties is a subscriber to the service.

For simplicity we assume that netting does not take place for this transaction.

Settlement

Settlement is the next step of the FX spot trade lifecycle. Settlement requires that funds are transferred into the respective Nostro accounts of Big Bank and US Street by close of business on 12 January 2007, which is the value date. These funds have to be transferred and received before the cut-off times in the US and the UK.

The following are the raft of activities that would occur on 12 January 2007 in respect of settlement of the FX spot trade:

- US Street sends MT210 Swift message (notice to receive) to TDB bank to notify that the sum of 1,000,000 GBP is to be received from Big Bank on settlement of the trade.
- Big Bank would request TDB bank to credit US Street with the sum of 1,000,000 GBP on 12 of January 2007 (value date) with an MT202 Swift message.
- US Street would also send an MT202 to BOC bank to request the sum of 1,656,900 USD to be credited to Big Bank on the value date of 12 January 2007.
- TDB bank sends MT910 (confirmation of credit) followed by MT950 (statement of account) when the GBP funds are credited to US Street.
- BOC sends MT910 (confirmation of credit) followed by MT950 (statement of account) when the USD funds are credited to Big Bank.

Nostro Reconciliation

Nostro reconciliation can now commence once the funds have been credited to the respective internal Nostro accounts of Big Bank. The purpose is to ensure that the BOC bank has credited the right amount of funds in USD on the value date. The process is essentially a matching process to uncover errors in the transactions before they are picked up by US Street.

Accounting

Once the Nostro reconciliation is complete, the cash from the deal is posted to the general ledger in the debit and credit sections. The details of the accounting aspect with regards to the general ledger are outside the scope of this book.

The Profit and Loss (P&L) on the trade would also be determined by revaluation of the trade. To fully understand the determination of P&L, the concept of position keeping will be discussed.

Position keeping is carried out by the trader in Big Bank who keeps a deal blotter that would have an entry for details of the trades described above as follows:

Counterparty	USD bought(+) /sold(−)	Exchange rate	GBP sold (−) / bought (+)	Net GBP position
US Street	+1,656,900	1.6569	−1,000,000	− 1,000,000

A description of the columns in the blotter is as follows:

- **Counterparty** – an entry of the counterparty to the trade i.e. US Street.
- **USD bought (+)/sold(-)** – the amount of the counter currency.
- **Exchange rate** – the exchange rate at which the deal was struck.
- **GBP sold(-)/bought(+)** – the amount of base currency.
- **Net GBP position** – the net sterling position for spot delivery of the base currency.

* It is assumed that the starting position for GBP was 0 in the trader's book.

To determine P&L the trader has to revalue the trade based on a revaluation or mark-to-market rate from the market. Often this rate is the mid-rate i.e. the halfway of the bid and offer rate.
The P&L for the trade can be determined as follows.

For illustration we will take a revaluation rate of 1.6566, at this rate this is a profit.

Profit (dollars) = 1,000,000 *(1.6569 − 1.6566) = USD 400
Profit (pounds) = 400/1.6569 = GBP 241.41.

Counterparty	USD bought(+) /sold(−)	Exchange rate	GBP sold (-) /bought (+)	Net GBP position	P&L USD	P&L GBP
US Street	+1,656,900	1.6569	+1,000,000	+1,000,000	400	241.41

The convention in the financial markets is that if the trader buys at a rate above the mid-rate, the entry in the blotter is denoted as a loss; if he sells above the mid-rate, the entry is denoted as a profit.

Problem Resolution and Investigation
Problems that are encountered in the FX spot trade lifecycle would be investigated and resolved before the cash from the trade is entered into the general ledger. Typical problems that are encountered in the trading lifecycle include:

- mismatch in the trade details during confirmation;
- error found in Nostro reconciliation;

- static data errors for currency pairs being traded;
- verification errors found during settlement.

In some instances the trade would be amended or cancelled and reissued depending on the nature of the trade. Different trading systems have different methods for maintaining the audit trail of a trade; while some systems keep a record of the cancelled trade some overwrite the details of the previous trade with the reissued trade.

Management

The management of the FX spot trade lifecycle is based on exception reporting of activities that occur during the lifecycle. The aim is to ensure that regulatory and statutory issues of the domiciliary country are complied with and reported accordingly. The following are some of the regulatory issues that the management activities encompass:

- foreign currency exposure
- capital adequacy
- back-office code of conduct
- money-laundering procedures.

Common Systems used in the Industry

This chapter describes some of the common systems used in the investment banking industry, the products that are traded with the systems, the functionality and some of the banks that have implemented them.

Introduction

With international markets in constant flux and exchanges modifying their electronic environments, investment banks in the global market need cost-effective and modular solutions, with multi-market, multi-instrument capabilities. Regulatory authorities are also pushing for more transparency and the financial industry is pushing for efficiency, especially where STP (straight-through processing) and automation are concerned. Investment banks have to deploy the best-of-breed solutions in the market to remain competitive and mitigate the risk of breaching the compliance rules of the regulators.

Systems that are used for front-, middle- and back-office activities in investment banks are usually developed by in-house technology staff. However, in recent times some application vendors have been dominating the investment banking market for off-the-shelf and custom-built applications to support the business processes across the asset classes.

Selection Criteria

When choosing applications and middleware to deploy, banks usually select a set of criteria to be met before committing to a purchase. The following table is a guide to a selection method that can be adopted.

For example, let's assume that a system called Bizasset is being considered.

Table 7.1 Selection Criteria for applications to be deployed in Investment Banking

Feature	Weighting	Score	Points Allocated
Products traded	3	8	24
Ease of development of API	2	6	12
STP capabilities	2	7	14
Ease of navigation	2	7	14
Number of trade capture fields	3	8	24
Ease of integration with existing systems	3	9	27
Customer support	3	8	24
Cost of deployment	1	6	6
Real-time capability	2	4	8
Scalability	3	9	27
Total			180

The weighting could be on a scale of 1 through 3. The score would be on a scale of 1 through 10.

Points would be allocated as score * weighting and the total number of points would determine the eventual selection. In this case, with a score of 180, Bizasset would be the system of choice ahead of other systems that were considered which scored less.

Notable Applications used in Investment Banking

The following are descriptions of the more common systems developed by application vendors and used by most of the major investment banks.

Calypso

Calypso Technology, Inc. provides the Calypso suite of solutions for capital markets trading. Calypso is a fully integrated front-to-back software system which enables trading, P&L and position management, integrated cross-asset risk management and straight-through processing.

The key differentiator of Calypso is its underlying software technology. Built using modern design and development techniques, Calypso is a scalable solution in that the process of adding new products, models, etc. is simplified and it has the capacity to support increases in trade volumes.

Calypso covers numerous products under the following groups:

- foreign exchange
- foreign exchange derivatives
- money markets
- fixed income
- interest rate derivatives
- hybrid products
- credit derivatives
- equities
- equity derivatives
- commodities.

The unique functions of Calypso

- Workflow – Calypso's workflow is designed for configurability to allow the required degree of STP.
- Structuring capabilities – Calypso eXSP enables the structuring of hybrid products linked to multiple underlying assets.
- Credit derivatives – Calypso's credit derivatives solution is considered to be the market-leading solution, based on the functionality for structured credit and the way in which it keeps pace with market developments.

The following banks use Calypso:

- HSBC
- Dresdner Kleinwort Wasserstein
- BNP Paribas
- Citigroup
- Bear Stearns
- RBS Financial Markets
- HVB
- Rabobank
- Calyon
- Rand Merchant Bank
- Sumitomo Trust & Banking
- Standard Bank.

Fidessa

Fidessa is developed and sold by Royal Blue group plc. It is an integrated suite of functional applications that manage and automate the front- and mid-office business flows of investment banks. Fidessa functionality encompasses:

- order management;
- electronic trading on major stock markets in Europe, Asia and America;
- risk and position management;
- trade confirmation.

The Fidessa trading platform provides an integrated suite of functional applications for sell-side firms trading equities in the US, European, Japanese and Asian markets. The Fidessa trading platform is available on a bespoke enterprise basis or as a fully hosted ASP solution.
Features include:

- remote service provider services
- ADR & GDR trading
- IOIs & trade adverts
- direct market access (directed flow)
- list management
- access to ECNs and ATSs
- post-trade support for order allocation
- VWAP (algorithmic) trading.

Fidessa is used in most banks primarily for equities trading. Dresdner Kleinwort Wasserstein, Commerzebank and Casenoze are some of the investment banks that use Fidessa.

Openlink

Endur

Endur is OpenLink's front- through back-office solution for trading, risk management and operations' needs in various commodity markets. Built on OpenLink's NGX Framework, Endur is a comprehensive solution serving markets in electricity, natural gas and natural gas liquids, crude oil and refined products, precious and base metals, weather derivatives, commodities and foreign exchange.

Endur links front, middle and back offices with functionality that was expressly designed to cover the entire transaction lifecycle. All information moves in real time in a straight-through-processing environment. That gives greater control over the risk connected with each and every transaction.

Powerful, integrated and efficient, Endur combines analytics with intricate pricing curves that help to relate the true value of any energy instrument. From deal capture to trade validation, processing, accounting, and settlement, Endur provides live data feeds featuring real-time position tracking pages that display up-to-the-second views of all exposures of every deal.

Barclays Capital is one of the investment banks that are using the Endur service for energy trading.

Findur

Findur links front, middle and back offices with functionality that was expressly designed to cover the entire transaction life cycle of a deal. All transactions are processed in real time in a straight-through-processing environment, giving the banks greater control over market, credit and operation/processing environments, including inherent risks and limits.

The following are the features of Findur that are designed to meet banks' business and technical requirements:

- powerful analytics
- real-time capability
- performance and flexibility
- broad asset class coverage
- transparency and security
- scalability
- efficiency
- cutting-edge technology.

The following products are traded in Findur:

- Spot FX
- FX Forwards
- Commercial Paper
- Certificate of Deposit
- FX Options.

Findur is used by most of the major investment banks including West LB Panmure, Deutsche Bank, Bank of America and Calyon.

SAP for Banking

SAP Accounting for Financial Instruments is designed specifically to help banks prepare for and meet IAS regulations, especially IAS 39.

SAP Accounting for Financial Instruments is used to prepare a local IAS-compliant financial report and create a parallel financial statement based on a central data pool fed from a bank's existing system landscape. For IAS-relevant business transactions, IAS-compliant values are calculated and these values replace the original results in the local financial report.

This technique avoids parallel and redundant data storage. Values are replaced only if the results in the local financial report differ from the IAS figures. Finally, the original data that complies with IAS – and the newly calculated IAS results – is consolidated according to the bank's reporting requirements and analysed by using SAP Business Intelligence. This data can be exported for further processing in other applications as needed.

Furthermore, with SAP Accounting for Financial Instruments a bank can address the IAS regulatory challenge within the fuller context of enterprise management. Designed around a central data pool and standardised methods, the solution for IAS can be seamlessly integrated into an efficient overall enterprise management solution.

SAP For Banking is used by banks such as Drkw, BNP Paribas and UBS.

GL Stream

GL Stream™ Workstation is GL TRADE's multi-asset front end designed for Proprietary and Agency trading firms. It offers speed, control, flexibility and multiple exchange connections via a single workstation – giving professional traders and market makers the definitive edge.

The GL Stream™ WS offers a variety of features to suit all types of trading activities: from simple buy and sell needs to highly automated and complex strategies via order capture, monitoring and routing across multiple liquidity pools.

Features
- Client order capture from multiple sources.
- Order routing to multiple liquidity pools including exchanges, market makers, brokers or third-party algorithmic trading services.
- Calculation of positions at every book hierarchy level in real time and across multiple venues.
- Automated trading without the programming giving traders time and price advantage on all equities and listed futures and options:

- program and combo trading
- automated trading
- options trading and market making
- futures SpreadMatrix engine
- spreadsheet trading
- market depth trading tool through powerful ladder
- options pricer
- pre-programmed tactics.

GL Stream WS can handle over 120 equities and derivatives markets worldwide.

Deutsche Bank, Calyon, Bear Stearns and Lehman Brothers are among the banks that use GL Stream.

Reuters Kondor+

Kondor+ is a deal capturing, position keeping and pricing system that offers a sophisticated and flexible means of managing deals and positions across all instruments in real time. It has proven itself in daily operation for more than 500 financial institutions in financial centres worldwide, across 14,000 positions in more than 60 countries – ranging from single-site installations to global rollouts at top-tier banks.

With market-standard pricing libraries from NumeriX and a host of new features, in its latest version Kondor+ offers comprehensive coverage of all instruments – from vanilla assets to exotic derivatives and structured products – all in one system. Its Kondor Open Trade and API module allows traders to access proprietary models and design tailor-made products with the help of a flexible, user-friendly toolkit.

Benefits
- Manages positions and their associated risk in real time.
- Allows the trader to enter own instruments to stay on top of the markets.
- Enables the pricing of positions correctly using NumeriX financial libraries.
- Increases efficiency by reducing the need for manual input.
- Enables straight-through processing by integrating with Reuters or third-party solutions.

Features
- Multiple asset support.
- Flexible pricing and deal management.
- Reporting and desktop analytics.
- Trade automation.

Reuters Kondor+ is used by most of the major investment banks such as Goldman Sachs and Merrill Lynch.

Sophis Risque

Built on 15 years' collaboration with 50 of the world's largest derivatives market makers, Sophis Risque is a comprehensive cross-asset, front-to-back office system for sell-side institutions. By focusing on the evolving needs of leading investment banks, Risque has developed into a fully adaptable and straight-through processing solution at the cutting edge of risk and portfolio management. This means Risque is ideally suited to support trading activities in high-volume listed markets and new kinds of exotic derivatives. The following instrument classes can be traded with Sophis Risque:

- equities and derivatives
- fixed income and interest rate derivatives
- credit derivatives
- commodities and derivatives
- FX derivatives
- structures and hybrids.

Sophis Risque references include the following:

- Abbey Financial Markets
- Barclays Capital
- BNP Paribas
- Fortis Bank
- HSBC
- HVB
- ING
- KBC
- Nomura Securities
- RaboBank.

Table 7.2 shows a list of other commonly used systems.

Middleware

Middleware, a term used to describe Enterprise Application Integration (EAI), has become widely accepted in investment banks as a necessary product throughout the industry. Trends in the industry such as the reduction in global trade-to-settlement times and the corresponding convergence of asset settlement methods require an environment in which the need to quickly and efficiently process data across a variety of different standards and protocols is essential and middleware has effectively supported these needs.

The selection criteria for middleware called MXasset are shown in Table 7.3.

Table 7.2 Commonly used systems

System	Uses
Anvil ARTS	Repos and Securities Lending
Murex	Cross Asset class trading and Risk Management
Tenemos Barracuda	Basel 2 Compliance
Reuters 3000 Xtra (hosted and deployed)	High-speed information service
Globus T24	Cross Asset class trading and Risk Management
Misys EagleEye	Trading Compliance
FinCad – The Perfect Hedge	IAS39 Hedge Effectiveness and Risk Management
FlexCube Nostro	Nostro Reconciliation
HotScan	Anti-Money Laundering
Misys Summit	Multiple asset class trading
SmartstreamTLM	Reconciliation, Investigations and Corporate Actions
Fermat	IAS 39 Compliance
IT & e Razor	Credit and Market Risk Management
Algo Collateral	Collateral management
Reuters Messaging	Instant messaging service for financial markets
Gresham's Real time Nostro	Nostro account management service
Sungard Martini	Securities Lending and Repo trading
Asset Control AC Plus	Reference data management

Table 7.3 Selection Criteria for Middleware be deployed in Investment Banking

Feature	Weighting	Score	Points Allocated
Throughput	3	9	27
Integration with existing software	3	7	21
Integration with external networks	2	6	12
Availability of upgrades	1	7	7
Ease of installation	2	6	12
Ease of Integration with existing systems	3	9	27
Customer support	1	7	7
Cost of deployment	2	8	16
Integration with standards	2	9	18
Scalability	3	9	27
		Total	174

The weighting could be on a scale of 1 through 3. The score would be on a scale of 1 through 10.

Points would be allocated as score * weighting and the total number of points would determine the eventual selection. In this case, with a score of 174,

MXasset would be the system of choice ahead of other middleware products that were considered which scored less.

In recent times, the following technological changes have affected the market for middleware products for investment banking:

- Automating and modifying internal trade workflow.
- Pressure to improve matching and reconciliation.
- Integration with multiple matching utilities.
- Integrating the investment process.
- Improved service levels to customers.
- Converting batch processes to real time.
- Standardisation of reference data and adopting industry standards.

Table 7.4 shows notable middleware products used in investment banking.

Table 7.4 Common Vendors and their Middleware used in Investment Banking

Middleware	Vendor
Mercator	GSS
MQ	IBM
MINT	Sungard
TIBCO	Rendezvous
Heliograph	Heliograph
Dovetail	Dovetail
Trade Suite	Omgeo
BizTalk	Microsoft
Coppelia	Javelin
e*Gate	SeeBeyond
Tuxedo	BEA

Mapping of Software Development Lifecycle to the Trading Lifecycle

8

This chapter covers the mapping of the development lifecycle to the trading lifecycle and a description of the work tasks involved in the mapping exercise.

Introduction

The activities that make up the trading lifecycle require some specific activities to ensure the delivery of high-quality systems. As a consequence, mapping of these activities to the software development lifecycle should be discussed to ensure that readers gain an understanding of what is required.

The Development Lifecycle

Figure 8.1 Software development lifecycle

As discussed in Chapter 5, the trading lifecycle is made up of activities from trade capture through to accounting. The mapping of the phases of the development lifecycle to the trading lifecycle is a worthwhile exercise that enables IT staff to prepare relevant tasks for developing an application for the lifecycle of trading.

It is worth noting that the work tasks described below are an estimation of the work tasks that are likely to be involved in these activities and do not represent the full range of tasks. Each system has its unique functional and technical requirements and as such each implementation team would need to carry out an assessment of the fit with their trading strategies and requirements.

Trade Capture (including verification)

Trade capture systems can be standalone systems that interface through a middleware to back office and accounting systems or can be part of a composite system that performs straight-through processing.

Scenario 1: Standalone trade capture system
In this scenario (see Table 8.1) there is usually a middleware that is an interface between the trade capture systems and the settlement system that converts the publishing message format to that of the subscriber settlement system.

Scenario 2: Trade capture as part of a Composite system
In this scenario (see Table 8.2) the composite system is usually an "out-of-the-box" solution with relatively minimal customisation. There is usually no requirement for a middleware to convert the format of the published messaging to that of the subscribing system.

Table 8.1 Work Tasks for Standalone Trade Capture systems

Work Tasks	Description	Relevant Lifecycle stage
Business Analysis		
Project initiation	Scoping of the project to implement the systems, organisation and risk assessment	Concept
Cost/benefit analysis	Analysis in quantitative terms of the outcome of the investment being made in the system	Concept
Requirements engineering	Gathering of requirements from the business user i.e. front and middle-office staff and design of requirements specification	Requirements
Functional design and specification	Functional design specification including process and data modelling	Design
Systems Analysis		
Interface designs	Design of the interfaces between the middleware and the trade capture system	Design
Design of customisation elements	Design of customisation elements if required	Design
Development		
APIs development	Development effort for the API to the trade capture systems	Code
Development of customisation elements	Development of customisation elements if required	Code
Unit testing	Full unit testing of the system	Test
Testing		
Integration testing	Integration test planning and execution performed with confirmation messages and the middleware	Test
Systems testing	Systems test planning and execution after the settlement, middleware and accounting systems are connected	Test
User acceptance testing (UAT)	UAT test planning and execution	Test
Implementation		
End-user training	Training the business users	Operation and maintenance
Deployment	Deployment into the live environment	Operation and maintenance
Application support	Support of the system in the live environment	Operation and maintenance

Table 8.2 Work Tasks for Trade Capture system as a part of Composite System

Work Tasks	Description	Relevant Lifecycle stage
Business Analysis		
Project initiation	Scoping of the project to implement the systems, organisation and risk assessment	Concept
Cost/benefit analysis	Analysis in quantitative terms of the outcome of the investment being made in the system	Concept
Requirements engineering	Gathering of requirements from the business user i.e. front and middle-office staff and design of requirements specification	Requirements
Functional design and specification	Functional design specification including process and data modelling	Design
Systems Analysis		
Design of customisation elements	Little, if any required. Possibly design of customisation elements	Design
Development		
Development of customisation elements	Development of customisation elements if required	Code
Unit testing	Partial unit testing of the customised elements	Test
Testing		
Integration testing	Integration test planning and execution performed with confirmation messages and SSIs	Test
Systems testing	"Straight-through" end-to-end system test planning and execution	Test
UAT	UAT test planning and execution	Test
Implementation		
End-user training	Training the business users	Operation and maintenance
Deployment	Deployment into the live environment	Operation and maintenance
Application support	Support of the system in the live environment	Operation and maintenance

Confirmation

As mentioned earlier, the confirmation process involves sending and receiving SWIFT messages and in most banks confirmation is already part of an existing framework. However, if it is to be customised to suit the requirements of the implementation of a new system or to accommodate more traded products, then Table 8.3 shows the most likely work tasks involved.

Table 8.3 Work Tasks for Confirmation System

Work Tasks	Description	Relevant Lifecycle stage
Business Analysis		
Project initiation	Scoping of the project to implement the systems, organisation; risk assessment, if deemed necessary	Concept
Requirements	Gathering of requirements from the business users i.e. front-, middle- and back-office staff	Requirements
Systems Analysis		
Layout designs	Design of the layout of the newly accommodated SWIFT messages	Design
Development		
Customisation of system	Development of customisation of systems to accommodate new messages	Code
Unit testing	Partial unit testing	Test
Testing		
Integration	Planning and execution of integration tests regarding the customisation	Test
Systems testing	System test planning and execution	Test
UAT	UAT test planning and execution	Test
Implementation		
Deployment	Training of the business users	Operation and maintenance
Application support	Deployment into the live environment	Operation and maintenance
Application support	Support of the system in the live environment	Operation and maintenance

Settlement (including netting)

As with trade capture systems, settlement systems can be standalone or part of a composite trading system. The scenarios for settlement systems like trade capture systems are as follows.

Scenario 1: Standalone settlement system

In this scenario there is usually a middleware that is an interface between the trade capture systems and the settlement system that converts the publishing message format to that of the subscriber settlement system.

Table 8.4 Work Tasks for Standalone Settlement system

Work Tasks	Description	Relevant Lifecycle stage
Business Analysis		
Project initiation	Scoping of the project to implement the systems, organisation; risk assessment, if deemed necessary	Concept
Cost/benefit analysis	Analysis in quantitative terms of the outcome of the investment being made in the system	Concept
Requirements	Gathering of requirements from the business user i.e. back-office staff and design of requirements specification	Requirements
Functional design and specification	Functional design specification including process and data modelling	Design
Systems Analysis		
Interface designs	Development of customisation elements if required	Design
Design of customisation elements	Design of customisation elements if required	Design
Development		
API development	Development effort for the API to the settlement systems	Code
Development of customisation elements	Development of customisation elements if required	Code
Unit testing	Full unit testing of the system	Test
Testing		
Integration	Integration test planning and execution performed with confirmation messages and the middleware	Test
Systems testing	Systems test planning and execution after the trade capture, middleware and accounting systems are connected	Test

UAT	UAT test planning and execution	Test

Implementation

End-user training	Training the business users	Operation and maintenance
Deployment	Deployment into the live environment	Operation and maintenance
Application support	Support of the system in the live environment	Operation and maintenance

Scenario 2: Settlement system as part of Composite system

In this scenario the composite system is usually an "out-of-the-box" solution with relatively minimal customisation. There is usually no requirement for a middleware to convert the format of the published messaging to that of the subscribing system. The work task for the settlement element of the composite system is shown in Table 8.5.

Table 8.5 Work Tasks for Settlement system as a part of Composite System

Work Tasks	Description	Relevant Lifecycle stage
Business Analysis		
Project initiation	Scoping of the project to implement the systems, organisation; risk assessment, if deemed necessary	Concept
Cost/benefit analysis	Analysis in quantitative terms of the outcome of the investment being made in the system	Concept
Requirements	Gathering of requirements from the business user i.e. back-office staff and design of requirements specification	Requirements
Functional design and specification	Functional design specification including process and data modelling	Design
Systems Analysis		
Design of customisation elements	Design of customisation elements	Design
Development		
Development of customisation elements	Development of customisation elements	Code
Unit testing	Partial unit testing of the system	Test

Testing

Integration testing	Integration test planning and execution performed with relevant "settlement" messages and SSIs	Test
Systems testing	"Straight-through" end-to-end system test planning and execution	Test
UAT	UAT test planning and execution	Test

Implementation

End-user training	Training the business users	Operation and maintenance
Deployment	Deployment into the live environment	Operation and maintenance
Application support	Support of the system in the live environment	Operation and maintenance

Accounting

Accounting systems are usually already part of the trading systems framework and so the work tasks involved in a new implementation/upgrade would likely be as shown below.

Table 8.6 Work Tasks for Accounting System

Work Tasks	Description	Relevant Lifecycle stage
Business Analysis		
Project initiation	Scoping of the project to implement the systems, organisation; risk assessment, if deemed necessary	Concept
Cost/benefit analysis	Analysis in quantitative terms of the outcome of the investment being made in the system	Concept
Requirements	Gathering of requirements from the business users i.e. back-office and accounting staff	Requirements
Functional design and specification	Functional design specification including process and data modelling	Design
Systems Analysis		
Interface designs	Design of the interfaces between the back office and the accounting systems	Design
Development		
Development of interfaces	Development of interfaces between the back office and the accounting systems	Code
Unit testing	Partial unit testing	Test

Testing

Integration	Integration test planning and execution (with interfaces depending on how environment is set up)	Test
Systems testing	"Straight-through" end-to-end system test planning and execution	Test
UAT	UAT test planning and execution	Test

Implementation

End-user training	Training the business users	Operation and maintenance
Deployment	Deployment into the live environment	Operation and maintenance
Application support	Support of the system in the live environment	Operation and maintenance

IT Project Types and Data Requirements

This chapter covers the list of common IT projects implemented in investment banks and the data requirements.

Introduction

The IT projects that are undertaken in the banks are usually greenfield implementations or upgrades to existing systems. The projects are usually instigated as a result of new changes in regulations or to maintain compliance to existing regulations. Other projects are carried out to remain competitive in a market space or to accommodate changes in the trading strategies for certain asset classes.

Common Types of IT Projects

Some common types of IT projects are:

- change management programmes
- business process reengineering projects
- implementation of new trading systems
- upgrades to existing trading systems
- implementation of risk management systems
- development of interfaces to systems
- integration of in-house systems to ASPs (application service providers)
- implementing trade data warehousing
- implementation of reporting systems
- data migration
- implementation of CRM systems
- implementation of ERP systems
- connection to ECN (electronic communication networks).

Others are:

- systems cutover
- implementation of portals
- compliance projects
- data normalisation projects
- upgrades to infrastructure
- upgrades to desktop
- desktop integration
- upgrade to accounting systems
- implementation of disaster recovery procedures.

Data Requirements

Data requirements to be discussed in this section cover the role of market and reference data in the trading environment and also information management as it relates to pre- and post-trade analysis and quantitative analysis.

97

Market Data

Market data is the barometer that traders in investment banks use for pricing their trades i.e. an information source for the trading community to gain an understanding of what their counterparts are quoting for the instruments they are trading.

What is Market Data?

Market data refers to quote- and trade-related data disseminated from equity, fixed-income, derivatives, currency or other exchanges. Market data may refer generically to data both directly originating from an exchange and derived from the underlying instruments (e.g. indices). While market data generally refers to real-time or delayed quotations, the domain can broadly exclude static or reference data relating to these instruments (e.g. CUSIP, which exchange a security trades on, end-of-day pricing etc). This data is generally captured and furnished to users via large-scale enterprise systems, in either a request-response or streaming manner. These systems often integrate with more pervasive middleware APIs such as Tibco.

Reuters and Bloomberg are the foremost providers of market data to most investment banks.

Historical Market Data

Historical market data is market data that is used for historical valuation. Historical market data is gathered from the world's exchanges and OTC (over-the-counter) markets. The following are examples of categories of historical market data:

- cash
- future prices
- forward points
- swaps points
- FX spots
- discount factors
- index fixings.

Others are country-specific historical data such as USD Crude Oil and Gold and GBP and EUR interest rate volatilities used for swaptions, and options calculations.

Companies such as FINCAD and Vhayu are providers of historical market data.

Market Data Systems

Market data systems are used mainly for the purpose of intelligent gathering. By definition, market data systems are systems that integrate, distribute and add value to information from markets, about the markets and affecting the markets.

Market information includes real-time and historical prices from order-driven trading venues, real-time and historical news from the press, the web and internal analysts, as well as internal calculations and other forms of proprietary information used to support crucial decisions.

Direct Data Feed
Investments banks are currently demanding direct data feeds as a result of consolidation in the financial markets and the need for fast access to execution destinations. A number of vendors including Reuters have developed low-latency direct data feeds.

Market Data Definition Language
One of the most recent developments in the market data arena is Market Data Definition Language (MDDL). There is a buzz in the investment banking industry about MDDL as it provides a language that "institutionalises" the formats and definitions of financial market intelligence.

What is MDDL?
MDDL is an XML-based interchange format and common data dictionary on the fields needed to describe:

- financial instruments
- corporate events affecting value and tradability
- market-related, economic and industrial indicators (MDDL.org).

MDDL was developed with the aim of getting entities to exchange market data by standardising formats and definitions. As it is based on XML, it is a common format for market data transmission between processing systems. It can be described as an open standard with a focus on interoperability.

Reference (Static) Data

Definition of reference data
Reference data is the set of underlying data elements used for executing trades in investment banks that consists of information such as counterparty details, instrument details, nature of the trade and conditions for settlement.

Reference data can be categorised into securities reference data and entities reference data. Securities data includes elements such as instrument identifiers, fixed income attributes, historical prices, tax rates, currency codes and exchange codes. Entity reference data consists of elements such as entity identifiers, account numbers, contact data and credit profiles.

Other Types of Reference data
The following are the types of data that are usually gathered for both functional and performance requirements:
- counterparty data – items such as counterparty name and credit and country ratings;

- currency pairs – static data items for base and counter currencies;
- currencies – such as spot rate and forward rates;
- portfolio – the names that have been assigned to the portfolio;
- book name – internal and external book names;
- holiday calendars – calendars for different currencies;
- interest basis – data that pertains to rate conventions e.g. ACT/365;
- contractual data – netting agreement, credit support agreement;
- futures exchanges – exchanges that futures contracts are traded on e.g. Euronext.Liffe;
- countries – names of countries for credit rating purposes;
- users – usernames of the users that access a system;
- groups – the business area that users belong to, for example compliance.

Reference Data Management

Reference data management focuses on the management of reference data that is shared by several disparate systems. The main business driver for reference data management is the growing importance of STP. However, the poor quality of reference data has destroyed many STP initiatives during the last decade.

The following are the benefits of reference data management:

- centralising data management
- efficient risk management
- reduction of reconciliation exceptions
- compliance with regulatory requirements.

Others are:

- reduction of the cost of error rectification
- improving response time to market opportunities
- reduction of duplicate and redundant data.

The current global regulatory landscape means that investment banks are now focusing on reference data management to reduce the risks associated with inconsistent and redundant data in their systems.

Information Management

Information management is another area of data management in investment banking that needs to be discussed owing to the growing importance of data handling in the competitive environment that these banks operate in. Volatility of the financial markets and a rapid succession of world-changing events have brought renewed attention to the importance for survival in the investment banking market space.

Definition

Information management is the handling of information (data) acquired by one or many disparate sources in a way that optimises access by all who have a share in that information or a right to that information.

In investment banking, information management involves capturing and analysing streaming real-time and historical data for algorithmic execution, testing of trading strategies, providing pre- and post-trade analysis and ensuring best execution compliance.

Case Study of Information Management

A case study of information management is carried out in this section using Reuters Tick Capture Engine (RTCE) as the vehicle for information management in investment banking.

What is Reuters Tick Capture Engine?

Reuters Tick Capture Engine is a system developed by Reuters for investment banks to facilitate pre-trade and post-trade analysis in search of best execution by analysing the market data update stream and, in parallel, store massive amounts of tick-by-tick, real-time and historical data. It captures real-time, historical and corporate action data in a central location, making it possible to query massive quantities of data for quantitative analysis and compliance.

RTCE meets the needs of banks in regards to pre-trade and post-trade analysis, algorithmic trading and quantitative analysis.

Pre-Trade Analysis

Overview of Pre-Trade Analysis

Pre-trade analysis in investment banking involves analysing potential trade opportunities by scanning market data in real time for conditions that meet a trading strategy. Investment banks deploy applications that poll major market centres for real-time prices and unusual trading activity, which can signify an important trend or event. These prices and unusual trading activities are the basis for formulating trading strategies.

The following are examples of trading strategies that are formulated using pre-trade analysis:

- statistical arbitrage
- index arbitrage
- basket trading
- transaction cost analysis using volume-weighted average price (VWAP).

How banks use RTCE for Pre-Trade Analysis

Investment banks use RTCE for processing and handling streaming market data and historical data for pre-trade analysis. RTCE calculates algorithms to perform the analysis and the output is communicated to traders to enable them to react quickly (in milliseconds) to market conditions and execute algorithmic strategies in a timely manner.

Market Trends

The advent of pre-trade analytics built with proprietary algorithms has aided investment bank traders in determining the expected market impact of potential trades. Traders are now empowered in this age of electronic trading to predict the potential future outcome of trades instead of having to share assumptions on market impact with the sales traders.

Post-Trade Analysis

Post-trade analytics is simply about the comparison between the expected and the actual outcome of trades with a view to making better trading decisions. Brokers in investment banks use post-trade analytics as a tool to measure how well a portfolio is managed.

Transaction cost analysis (TCA) is the bedrock of post-trade analysis that helps banks to determine the total cost of trade decisions. Post-trade analytics provides a holistic approach to TCA by comparing trades executed by the traders in the banks to the prevailing market conditions and a basis for aligning their strategic objectives accordingly.

An example of the benefits of post-trade analysis can be seen in the ease with which traders can change trading strategies in real time based on the feedback received from the post-trade analysis. Post-trade analysis allows an order to be reworked before it is completed, basing the revised order on a new strategy.

How Investment Banks use RTCE for Post-Trade Analysis

RTCE enables a customer to store almost any amount of market data for any amount of time. It combines streaming market data from major centres and other types of data like corporate action data from another Reuters product, Datascope Select, to create a customer-specific tick-by-tick database suitable for any type of post-trade analysis.

Market Trends

While investment banks are falling over themselves to get into transaction cost research and there is a burgeoning business in predicting what a trade should cost and where it would be analysed (pre-trade analytics), its is equally important these days to examine how well that strategy has been implemented by comparing the results to various benchmarks (post-trade analytics).

Algorithmic Trading

Algorithmic trading is the machine-driven approach to trading that entails placing a buy or sell order of a defined quantity into a quantitative model that generates the timing of orders based on goals specified by the parameters and constraints of the algorithm. These algorithms are designed to meet a number of goals such as best execution, best price, mid price or minimal market impact.

How banks use RTCE for Algorithmic Trading

RTCE is used in the banks for comparing streaming market data in real time against historical data to calculate algorithms such as VWAP to transmit signals to traders or an order management system and store the market data well.

Market trends

The proliferation of trading algorithms created by the investment banks and VWAP is a driver in the rapid growth in electronic trading. Current research has revealed that the US is at the forefront of electronic trading and leveraging order management systems, while in Europe MiFID may act as a catalyst for algorithmic trading.

According to Reuters:

"Algorithmic trading has become a part of the mainstream in response to buy-side traders' need to move large blocks of shares with minimum market impact in today's complex institutional trading environment."

Quantitative analysis

Quantitative analysis is a business or financial analysis technique that is used in investment banks to identify investment opportunities by querying massive volumes of historical and market data. It is also employed to optimise trade execution.

Quantitative analysis in investment banking is a carried out by quantitative analysts, often referred to as "quants", who are highly skilled financial engineers with higher degrees in mathematics or statistics.

Examples of quantitative analysis include everything from simple financial ratios such as earnings per share, to something as complicated as discounted cash flow or option pricing. Other examples include building trading models that can anticipate price movements based on correlation and market conditions, and liquidity and impact analysis, which involves analysing the full historical depth of order books from selected market centres over time to uncover trends.

How banks use RTCE for Quantitative analysis

RTCE is used to analyse massive quantities of historical and real-time data to reduce time-to-market of new strategies the banks formulate in order to gain a competitive edge.

Market Trends

The following trends in the investment landscape are shaping the quantitative analysis discipline:

■ Advances in fixed income quantitative techniques – there is better transparency in the bond markets in terms of the quality and the availability for data on the behaviour of bonds. As a consequence, bonds and debt securities as a whole are becoming more amenable to the types of quantitative analysis that were traditionally used in equity markets.

103

■ The analysis of extreme events – quants are beginning to evaluate massive volumes of data to see how markets would behave if highly unlikely events were to occur.

Test Data

Test data used in investment banks usually comprises data that is processed from trade capture through to settlement and accounting. Test data allows test cases and scripts to be implemented and executed successfully. Test cases and scripts are merely descriptions of conditions, scenarios and paths and without test data there would be no concrete values to precisely identify them.

Test data is critical to the success of the deployment of applications in the investment banks as it can be manipulated to suit different conditions under which the application would be used. As seen in Chapter 7, the applications that are used in investment banking have complex functionality, hence the need to ensure that the data that is used for testing these systems reflects the market conditions and suits the business processes.

The following are key requirements and characteristics of test data:

■ data isolation
■ data re-use
■ data initial state repeatability
■ profiling
■ data cataloguing and enumeration
■ data safety
■ data version control.

Test data management
Test data management involves sets of activities and artefacts that are spread over the development lifecycle. The key to effective test data management is to start gathering test data in the early phases of a software development lifecycle.

The best practices of test data management are based on three pillars:

■ sampling
■ creation
■ maintenance.

Sanitising test data
Sanitisation of test data is carried out to ensure that data extracted from live systems for testing purposes is not exposed to unauthorised personnel. It entails changing certain attributes in the data sets whilst ensuring that the logic for processing the data is not compromised.

The sanitation of test data also takes the Data Protection Act of 1998 into consideration. The details of the data protection act can be found on the following url: http://www.opsi.gov.uk/acts/acts1998/19980029.htm

Data Volumes

A huge number of trades are booked daily in the different front-office systems in the banks. As a result, simulating the front-to-back processing of trades requires consideration of the volumes of data to be processed. Also to be considered is the timing of the data traffic as some global systems receive feeds from different time zones across the world.

Performance tests that are identified for these kinds of scenario have to be thoroughly planned and the appropriate testing tools adopted. The requirements for the throughput of data are clearly defined and metrics specified within a feasible range.

10

Terminology commonly used in the Investment Banking Industry

This chapter lists the terminology commonly used in the industry that IT professionals will come across in the course of the business day in the investment banks.

Introduction

The terminology used in investment banking is vast and varied owing to the complex nature of the activities in the industry. It is important for IT staff in general to have an appreciation of the terminology in order to converse freely with the business community and to build better systems that support the underlying business processes.

Some of the terms used in the industry are discussed below, but are by no means exhaustive. Further searches can be carried out on the Internet (www.Bizle.biz) or in textbooks and journals for other terms not covered in this section.

List of Terms

Accounts payable – Invoiced amounts owed by a bank to its creditors.

Accounts receivable – Invoiced amounts owed to a bank by its debtors.

Amortisation – The repayment of the principal of a loan in regular instalments over a period of time rather than all of it at the maturity of the loan.

Arbitrage – Buying and selling in different market places simultaneously and making risk-free profits from the disparity between marketplaces.

Asset class – A type of investment, such as stocks and bonds.

Backwardation – When the forward or future price of a commodity is less than the cash or spot price, i.e. the price of the future or forward price is higher in the near term than the longer term.

Basket trading – Basket trading is a single order to buy or sell a set of 15 or more securities by institutional investors to invest large amounts of money in a particular portfolio or index.

Basis point – In money and bond markets one basis point equals 0.01%.

Benchmark bond – A liquid government bond with a round maturity such as 10 years. Its price is actively followed in the market, i.e. it is the benchmark by which the performance of other bonds is measured.

Bid/offer spread – The difference between the highest price a trader will pay for buying an asset and the lowest price a seller wishes to sell at. In the money markets, it is the difference between the interest rate a trader pays for borrowing and lending funds.

Big figure – In the foreign exchange markets, the first decimal places of a currency rate quotation. For example, USD: EUR 1.5678/79.

Boutique – A small financial services firm that concentrates on a limited range of specialised activities for a select number of individuals.

Business day convention – A calendar convention used to determine the number of days between two coupon dates, which is used in calculating accrued interest or yield when the next coupon payment is less than a full coupon period away. Each bond market has its own day-count convention. For example, the day-count convention for commercial papers is 30/360.

Buy side – Non-brokerage firm (i.e. mutual fund or pension fund) which provides research and recommendations exclusively for the benefit of the company's own money managers (as opposed to individual investors).

Cable – The sterling-dollar exchange rate. It is so-called because deals used to be transacted through a transatlantic cable.

Call money – A deposit or loan that is repayable on demand.

Call option – An option contract that gives the holder the right to buy a certain quantity (usually 100 shares) of an underlying security from the writer of the option, at a specified price (the strike price) up to a specified date (the expiration date).

Cash settlement – Settling a contract in cash rather than through the physical delivery of an asset or commodity.

Clean price – The price of a bond excluding interest that has accrued since the last coupon date.

Coupon – The interest rate payable on a bond.

Cum dividend – The buyer of a cum-dividend security is entitled to the next dividend payment.

Dual listing – When a security is registered for trading on more than one exchange.

Dirty price – Pricing of bond to include accrued interest.

Down tick – When trading in a security happens to be at price below the previous trade.

Ex-dividend – The buyer of a security trading ex-dividend is not entitled to the next dividend. It goes to the seller.

Exchange-traded contract – A derivative contract traded on an exchange rather than over the counter.

Exercise – The action taken by the holder of a call (put) option (see option below) when he or she takes the option to buy (sell) the underlying asset.

Face value – The principal or par value of a debt security such a bond or a treasury bill. Normally the face value is repaid at maturity.

Fair value – The theoretical value of a financial asset, often established using a pricing model.

Fill-or-kill (FOK) – A type of order on an exchange which is either executed at the stipulated price or cancelled.

Forward contract – An agreement to buy or sell a security, commodity or currency at an agreed price for delivery at some date in the future.

Forward exchange rate – The rate to exchange two currencies on a date later than spot.

Front running – When a trader creates a position on the trading book in anticipation of a large deal which may move the market.

Futures contract – An agreement transacted through an organised exchange to buy or sell a security or commodity at an agreed price for delivery in the future.

Gilt – A bond issued by the UK government.

Grey market – Trading in securities before they are issued.

Haircut – When securities are pledged as collateral against a loan, the lender will normally apply a "haircut" and lend less than their current market value.

Hard currency – Currency usually from a highly industrialised country that is widely accepted around the world.

Heating degree days – One of the most common types of weather derivative.

Hedging – Protecting against potential losses. For example, a borrower can buy a forward rate agreement as a hedge and will receive compensation payments if the interest rate rises.

In-the-money – An option that has intrinsic value.

Indexing – The weighting of the assets in a portfolio so that it matches that of an index.

Index arbitrage – An investment strategy that attempts to profit from the differences between actual and theoretical futures prices of the same stock index. This is done by simultaneously buying (or selling) a stock index future while selling (or buying) the stocks in that index.

Initial margin – A trader on a futures and options exchange has to deposit an initial margin as a performance deposit. This can be cash or (by agreement with the broker) some other acceptable collateral such as Treasury bills.

Institutional investor – A firm such as a pension fund investing money on behalf of other people.

LIBOR – London Inter-Bank Offer Rate. The interest rate that the banks charge each other for loans. This rate is applicable to the short-term international interbank market and applies to very large loans borrowed for anywhere from one day to five years.

Limit order – An order from a client to buy or sell a security or a futures or options contract where the client specifies a maximum purchase price or minimum sale price.

Long position or long – The position of a trader who has bought securities or futures or options contracts.

Margin trading – In some markets, such as the US, it is possible to buy shares "on margin" – that is by putting up a proportion of the purchase price and borrowing the rest from the broker.

Mark-to-market – Valuation of a security on a daily basis to calculate Profit and Losses (P&L).

Market maker – A brokerage or bank that maintains a firm bid and ask price in a given security by standing ready, willing and able to buy or sell at publicly quoted prices.

Net present value – NPV. The present value of an investment's future net cash flows minus the initial investment. If positive, the investment should be made (unless an even better investment exists), otherwise it should not.

Non-convertible currency – Any currency that is used primarily for domestic transactions and is not openly traded on a forex market. This is usually a result of government restrictions, which prevent it from being exchanged for foreign currencies.

Notional principal – In an interest rate swap, the specified dollar amounts on which the exchanged interest payments are based.

Off-balance-sheet – An item that does not appear in the assets or liabilities column on a company's balance sheet.

Open position – A long or short position in securities or other assets that is not yet closed out, which therefore gives rise to market or price risk until it is closed or hedged.

Option – The right but not the obligation to buy or sell a given security or commodity at a fixed price (the exercise or strike price).

Over-the-counter (OTC) transactions – Trades and deals that are agreed directly between parties rather through an exchange.

Par – The face or nominal value of a bond or bill, normally repaid at maturity. Bonds are quoted as a percentage of par.

Plain vanilla – The most standard form of a financial instrument, such as a straight coupon-paying bond with a fixed maturity.

Quote-driven market – A market in which market makers (traders) quote bid and offer prices for securities.

Repo rate – The rate of interest charged by the lender of funds in a repo.

Return-on-equity – Profit attributable to the ordinary shareholders as a proportion of the equity capital in the business.

Scrip dividend – When an investor takes a dividend in the form of new shares rather than cash.

Sell side – The brokerage and research departments of investment banks that sell securities and make recommendations for the bank's clients and the public.

Settlement of differences – With some derivatives contracts there is no physical delivery. The difference between the contract price and the price of the underlying asset is settled in cash.

Short position or short – Someone who has sold cash security they do not own.

Spot foreign exchange – The rate for exchanging two currencies.

Spot price – The price of a security for spot delivery. Also known as the "cash price".

Spread – The difference between two prices or rates.

Statistical arbitrage – Statistical arbitrage is a profit situation arising from pricing inefficiencies between securities using mathematical models.

Stock split – When a company thinks its share price is too unmanageable, it issues a number of new shares to replace the existing shares.

Stop-loss order – An order by a broker to close out a position and limit the losses whenever a given price level is reached.

Stop-profit order – An order by a broker to close out a position and take the profits to date whenever a given price level is reached.

Straddle – A combined option strategy which involves simultaneously selling a call and a put or buying a call and a put on the same underlying asset with the same strike and the same time to expiration.

Strangle – Like a straddle except the options used in the strategy have different strikes.

Strike price – Another term for the exercise price of an option.

Swap – A binding contract between two parties agreeing to make payments to each other on specified future dates over an agreed time period.

Tenor – Time to maturity.

Term deposit or loan – A deposit or loan with a specific maturity.

Tick size – The minimum price move allowed in a price quotation.

Two-way quotation – A dealer's bid and offer price.

Value at risk – A statistical estimate of the maximum loss that can be made on a portfolio of assets to ascertain confidence level and over a given period.

Variation margin – Additional margin paid or received when a derivatives contract is market-to-market and there is margin call from the clearing house.

Vostro account – A payment account maintained by a bank on behalf of another bank.

Yield – The return on an investment, taking into account the amount invested and the expected future cash flows.

Zero coupon bond – A bond which does not pay a coupon and which trades at a discount to its par of face value.

Methodologies, Skills and Tools

This chapter covers the methodologies, methods used and skills required to work in investment banking.

Introduction

The methodologies, skills and tools used in the investment banking industry will be discussed in this section to ensure that readers focus on what is required. There is a myriad of tools available in the market but the banks appear to standardise on specific tools and these tools are adopted in the majority of the investment banks. There are also specific skills that are required to carry out specific duties for projects in the banks.

Methodologies

In software engineering and project management, "methodology" is often used to refer to a codified set of recommended practices, sometimes accompanied by training materials, formal educational programmes, worksheets and diagramming tools. In investment banking, the best methodologies are employed to ensure that business-critical systems are built to a sufficient level of quality as required by the activities carried out in the industry.

V-Model
The V-model is a graphical representation of the system development lifecycle. It summarises the main steps to be taken in conjunction with the corresponding deliverables during the lifecycle.

Figure 11.1 V-Model

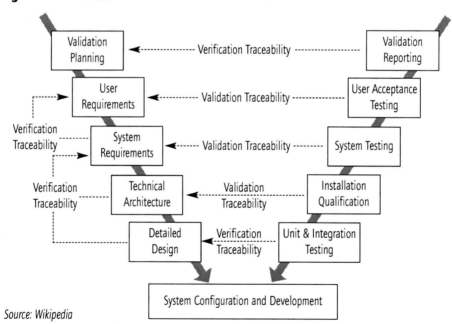

Source: Wikipedia

113

The left side of the V shows the specification stream where the system specifications are defined, while the right side of the V represents the testing stream where the systems are being tested (against the specifications defined on the left side). The base of the V, where the sides meet, represents the development stream.

RUP

The Rational Unified Process (RUP) is an iterative software development process created by the Rational Software Corporation, now a division of IBM. RUP is not a single concrete prescriptive process but rather an adaptable process framework. As such, RUP describes how to develop software effectively using proven techniques. While RUP encompasses a large number of different activities, it is also intended to be tailored, in the sense of selecting the development processes appropriate to a particular software project or development organisation. RUP is recognised as being particularly applicable to larger software development teams working on large projects.

Figure 11.2 RUP

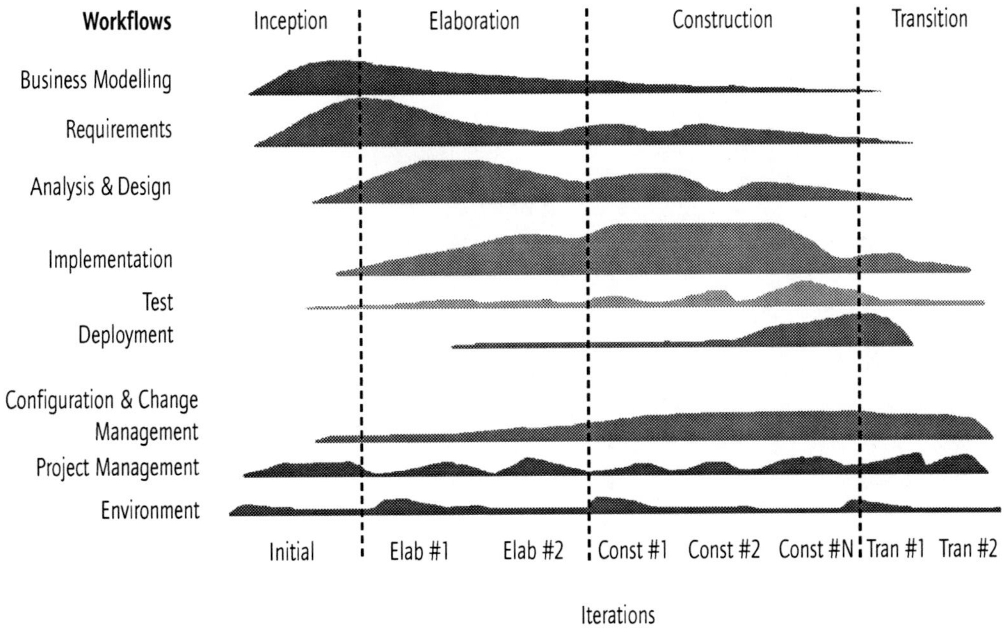

Source: Rational Software

Using RUP, software product lifecycles are broken into individual development cycles. These cycles are further broken into their main components, called phases. In RUP, these phases are termed as:

- inception phase
- elaboration phase
- construction phase
- transition phase.

Phases are composed of iterations. Iterations are timeboxes; iterations have deadlines while phases have objectives.

PRINCE2

Prince stands for Projects in Controlled Environments. Prince2 is the latest version of Prince, released in 1996, and is a project management methodology for the organisation, management and control of projects.

Figure 11.3 Prince2

The diagram below shows Prince2 processes. The arrows symbolise flows of information.

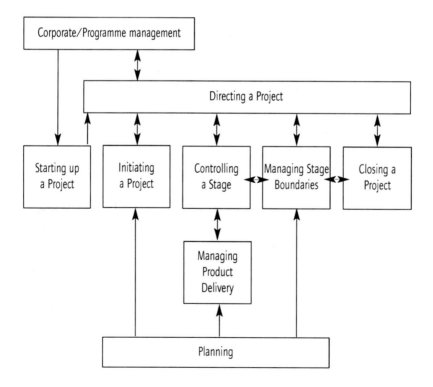

Source: Prince2 Handbook

Prince2 offers a process-based approach to key areas of project management. It is made up of eight high-level processes:

- directing a project (DP);
- planning (PL);
- starting up a project (SU);
- initiating a project (IP);
- controlling a stage (CS);
- managing product delivery (MP);
- managing stage boundaries (SB);
- closing a project (CP).

UML

The Unified Modelling Language (UML) is a non-proprietary, object modelling and specification language used in software engineering. The UML model can be used to showcase the functionality of a system, the structure and sub-structure and the internal behaviour. The following are artefacts that can be created using UML:

- use cases
- class diagrams
- sequence diagrams
- state activity diagrams.

RAD

Rapid Application Development (RAD) is a software development process that involves iterative development and the construction of prototypes.

Core Elements of RAD

RAD has six core elements:

- prototyping
- iterative development
- timeboxing
- team members
- management approach
- RAD tools.

Agile

Agile software development is a conceptual framework for undertaking software engineering projects. Agile methods attempt to minimise risk by developing software in short timeboxes, called iterations, which typically last one to four weeks. Each iteration is like a miniature software project of its own and includes all of the tasks necessary to release the mini-increment of new functionality: planning, requirements analysis, design, coding, testing and documentation. While iteration may not add enough functionality to warrant releasing the product, an agile software project intends to be capable of releasing new software at the end of every iteration. At the end of each iteration, the team re-evaluates project priorities.

Extreme Programming

Extreme Programming (XP) is a software engineering methodology for the development of software projects. It prescribes a set of day-to-day practices for developers and managers; the practices are meant to embody and encourage particular values and:

- involve new or prototype technology, where the requirements change rapidly, or some development is required to discover unforeseen implementation problems;
- are small and more easily managed though informal methods.

Pair Programming

Pair programming involves having two programmers working side by side, collaborating on the same design, algorithm, code or test. One programmer, the driver, has control of the keyboard/mouse and actively implements the program. The other programmer, the observer, continuously observes the work of the driver to identify tactical (syntactic, spelling, etc.) defects and also thinks strategically about the direction of the work. On demand, the two programmers can brainstorm any challenging problem. Because the two programmers periodically switch roles, they work together as equals to develop software.

Business and Systems Analysis Methods

Business and systems analysis methods adopted in the development of software in the investment banking industry are vast and varied but the following are the most commonly used.

Business rules approach

The business rules approach is a development methodology where rules are in a form that is used by but not embedded in business process management systems.

The business rules approach formalises an enterprise's critical business rules in a language the manager and technologist can understand. Business rules create an unambiguous statement of what a business does, with information to decide a proposition. The formal specification becomes information for process and rules engines to run.

Entity-relationship diagrams

The entity-relationship model or entity-relationship diagram (ERD) is a data model or diagram for high-level descriptions of conceptual data models and it provides a graphical notation for representing such data models in the form of entity-relationship diagrams. Such models are typically used in the first stage of information system design; they are used, for example, to describe information

117

needs and/or the type of information that is to be stored in the database during the requirements analysis.

Prototyping

The prototyping model is a software development process that begins with requirements collection, followed by prototyping and user evaluation. Often the end users may not be able to provide a complete set of application objectives, detailed input, processing or output requirements in the initial stage. After the user evaluation, another prototype will be built based on feedback from users and again the cycle returns to customer evaluation. The cycle starts by listening to the user, followed by building or revising a mock-up and letting the user test the mock-up, then it goes back to the beginning again.

Testing Methods

The following are common testing methods adopted in systems development in investment banking.

Equivalence Partitioning

Equivalence partitioning is a systematic process that identifies, on the basis of whatever information is available, a set of classes of input conditions to be tested. Each class is a representative of a large set of other possible tests.

Boundary Value Analysis

Boundary value analysis is a variant and refinement of equivalence partitioning with two major differences. First, rather than selecting any element in an equivalence class as being representative, elements are selected such that each edge of the equivalence class is the subject of a test.

Second, rather than focusing exclusively on input conditions, output conditions are also explored by defining output equivalent classes.

Error Guessing

Error guessing is an ad hoc approach, based on intuition and experience, to identifying tests that are considered likely to expose errors. The basic approach is to make a list of possible errors or error-prone situations and then develop tests based on the list.

Tools

Some of the most popular tools used in the investment banking industry for software development, project management, test management and defect tracking are listed below.

IBM Rational Rose

Rational Rose is an object-oriented, Unified Modelling Language (UML) software design tool intended for the visual modelling and component construction of enterprise-level software applications.

IBM Rational ClearCase

ClearCase provides life-cycle management and control of software development assets. It is used in the banks for change management and control of source code and artefacts.

Mercury QTP

This Mercury interactive test automation tool is used mainly in the banks for the automation of regression tests and data-driven tests.

IBM Rational ClearQuest

ClearQuest helps to automate and enforce development processes, manage issues throughout the project life cycle and facilitate communication between all stakeholders across the enterprise software. It is used in the banks for defect management and change tracking.

Mercury Test Director (Quality Centre)

This Mercury interactive test management tool is used in the banks for storing requirements, test cases and scripts. Test Director is fast becoming the industry standard for test management.

Oracle Designer

Oracle Designer offers a toolset to model, generate and capture the requirements and design of web-based applications quickly, accurately and efficiently, and also to assess the impact of changing those designs and applications.

PowerDesigner

PowerDesigner is a business process modelling approach to align business and IT, is an enterprise data modelling and database design solution that helps implement effective Enterprise Architecture and brings a powerful conceptual data model to the application development life cycle.

PowerDesigner uniquely combines several standard data modelling techniques (UML, Business Process Modelling and market-leading data modelling) together with leading development environments such as .NET, Workspace, PowerBuilder, Java, Eclipse, etc. to bring business analysis and formal database design solutions to the traditional software development lifecycle. Also, it works with all modern RDBMS.

Common IT Skills Required

IT professionals usually update their skills in line with technological advancements but to compete in the skills market in investment banking some specific skills are required in various capacities. These are some of the skills that employers in the industry demand:

- **JAVA** – experience and knowledge of Java Collections Classes, threads, swing development, design patterns, messaging middleware concepts.
- **C++** – experience and knowledge of C++ multi-threading, STL, design patterns, messaging middleware concepts.
- **BizTalk** – good knowledge of Microsoft BizTalk.
- **ControlM** – knowledge and experience of ControlM – a system that provides advanced production-scheduling capabilities across the enterprise from a single point of control – is desirable.
- **.NET** – experience and understanding of Web services – small, reusable applications that help computers from many different operating-system platforms work together by exchanging messages – from technical and business perspectives.
- **J2EE** (Java 2 Platform, Enterprise Edition) – appreciation and experience of this platform is essential.
- **Junit** – knowledge of Junit – a regression-testing framework used by the developer who implements unit tests in Java – is desirable.
- **Market Data** – ability to interpret the data feeds from providers like Reuters and Bloomberg.
- **XP** – proficiency in Microsoft XP is important.
- **Microsoft Excel** – it is essential to be proficient in Microsoft Excel. It is also desirable to have good skills in VBA.
- **Business Objects** – knowledge of Business Objects and the ability to manipulate data for reports in Business Objects is an essential skill to have.
- **UNIX** – it is essential to have knowledge and experience of UNIX and Linux and associated scripting languages.
- **SQL** – proficiency in writing SQL queries. Most banks use Sybase and Oracle databases, therefore it is vital to have a good command of PL/SQL and also TransactSQL, and tools such as TOAD and Oracle Discoverer.
- **IBM Websphere** – the ability to perform administrative tasks such as starting and stopping processes and deploying builds in IBM Websphere is essential.
- **Messaging platforms** – knowledge of IBM's MQ series, MINT, Tuxedo and Rendezvous ETX.
- **Cruise Control** – knowledge of Cruise Control is desirable. Cruise Control is usually used for deploying software builds.
- **FIX protocol** – at least a basic knowledge of FIX (Financial Information Exchange) protocol is desirable.
- **XML** – a rudimentary knowledge of XML is required to work successfully in IT in investment banking. Knowledge of the structure of XML messages is

important, especially the financial variants such as Fpml, FIXML, MDDL and NewsML.

■ **SWIFT** – understanding the format and categories of SWIFT messages.

■ **TIBCO** – good knowledge of TIBCO business process and optimisation software is desirable.

■ **ISO 15022** – knowledge of ISO15022 – principles necessary to provide the different communities of users with the tools to design message types to support their specific information flows – is important. It is necessary to understand the set of syntax and message design rules and the dictionary of data fields.

Soft Skills

■ **Numeracy** – having numerical skills is important if readers want to work on banking projects as there are usually complex calculations involved in developing and verifying the functionality of some applications.

■ **Business acumen** – a solid business acumen and awareness is required to perform well in the investment banking sector. Readers should make a habit of reading news in the financial pages of the broadsheets or periodicals such as The Economist.

■ **Good communication skills** – it is essential to be able to explain concepts in banking and finance from both a technical and business standpoint in order to gain the confidence of the business users.

■ **Business analysis skills** – the ability to understand business requirements and be able to document them is a nice skill to have. Readers should learn the art of extracting vital information from workshops and meetings with business users.

■ **Inductive thinking** – the ability to think inductively will stand readers in good stead.

■ **Good writing skills** – good writing skills are important in order to produce high-quality documentation.

■ **Ability to withstand pressure** – the work environment in the banking sector is highly pressurised and as such requires the ability to withstand pressure.

■ **Ability to see the "big picture"** – ability to see the bigger picture in order to understand the wider implications of the work tasks for the profitability of organisations.

■ **Basic understanding of economics** – a basic understanding of economics is required to work in the sector if readers want a fulfilling career in investment banking.

■ **Proficiency in different languages** – a proficiency in different languages would be beneficial as some of the projects could span different continents. The discerning IT professional should be able to communicate with business users and other IT professionals in another language.

■ **Negotiation skills** – good negotiation skills are important because of the aggressive deadlines to which projects are executed.

12

Conclusion

This chapter covers the future trends that might shape the business and IT in investment banking. It also provides a list of useful websites for readers.

The Future

What does it hold for investment banks in business and IT?

The investment banking industry is traditionally shaped by factors such as globalisation, demographics, regulation, risk and technology. Investment banks that are seeking to maintain their position in the increasingly competitive marketplace will be taking these into account in order to maintain strategic focus.

Investment banks will be looking into the future concentrating on the following key areas:

- exploitation of opportunities in new markets;
- implementation of new strategies for regulatory compliance;
- creation of frameworks for risk management;
- adoption of new technology.

Opportunities in new markets

Cross-border business opportunities will be the mainstay of the industry for years to come. Global investment banks such as HSBC are looking to expand their operations into newly developed and emerging markets. According to Deloitte:

> "HSBC projects that over the next 25 years much of the world's growth is coming from Asia, where it is making big investments, and the Americas, encouraged by the NAFTA agreement."

In Europe, examples such as the acquisition of Abbey in 2004 by Grupo Santander for $15.8 billion and UniCredito's $19 billion takeover of HypoVerinsbank in 2005*, have shown glimpses of the future outlook of the investment banking marketplace.

Outside Europe, China presents the biggest opportunities for investment banks to consolidate their global expansion strategies. Other markets include India, Korea, Taiwan and Singapore. According to Deloitte, Credit Suisse has identified six target Asian markets and is tailoring its strategy to each market. The bank formed a joint venture with Commercial Bank of China (CIBC) to offer mutual fund services for investing in stock and money markets.

---

* Figures were extracted from Deloitte Research report "A New Playing Field: Creating Global Champions".

123

New strategies for regulatory compliance

Regulatory compliance is one of the biggest issues that investment banks have to grapple with in the future. There is no bank that is above the regulations laid down by regulatory bodies, both locally and globally. As seen in previous chapters, there are a number of regulations such as Basel 2 and SOX that exist in the regulatory landscape which no bank can afford to ignore.

Given these existing and forthcoming regulations, investment banks will be adopting structured methodologies across business divisions and geographical boundaries to mitigate compliance risks by documenting these risks, introducing controls, and testing and implementing these controls using current and emerging technologies.

Frameworks for risk management

Risk management is one of the most common buzzwords in the marketplace. Investment banks have traditionally had frameworks in place to mitigate credit and market risks. However, operational risk is where the focus will be in the future. Notable operational risk failures such as the $355 million trade glitch in December 2005 by Japan's Mizouho Securities and the Tokyo Stock Exchange has exposed the weakness of banks in terms of coping with these types of risk.

According to Deloitte:

"Firms are turning to enterprise risk management (ERM), whose key components involve standardising the risk management process, aggregating a view of all risks and relating risk to business objectives."

This will be the case even more so in the future.

New Technology

Given the risk management, compliance and expansion issues that have been discussed, technology will be the cornerstone for realising these objectives. Increased spending on technology will be the key driver for sustaining competitive advantage and maintaining a presence in the marketplace.

It is an understated fact that technology is under-utilised in the banking world; the potential is huge and unrealised. The prediction is that electronic trading for institutions will predominate, with platforms that provide trading scenario analysis, risk modelling and performance management reporting. The electronic trading systems will be more advanced versions of the currently available multi-product electronic trading platforms that feature direct market access (DMA) and algorithmic trading.

Outsourcing to Cheaper Labour markets

The practice of outsourcing non-core functions to cheaper labour markets with the aim of realising cost savings is usually referred to as "offshoring". Investment banks are incorporating this into their overall strategies. For example, according to Deloitte, HSBC is currently offshoring IT development amongst other operations into, notably, India and other countries including Malaysia, the Philippines and Sri Lanka.

Industry experts predict that offshoring could yield up to 50% or more cost savings for the banks in the medium to long term.

Conclusion

The business of investment banking will be more global and the most successful players will perfect their strategies and establish themselves firmly and profitably in key overseas markets. There will be increased and sustainable consolidation in the European banking markets and there will be a greater drive to build a presence in China. Technology will be the bedrock of these strategies with increased spending on IT systems.

There will be limitless opportunities for IT professionals with the right business skills in the global investment banking industry. As discussed in the previous chapters, the industry has a lot of business divisions that are growing in leaps and bounds and will require the skills of IT professionals to operate efficiently for years to come.

Readers, after gleaning the information contained in this publication, should decide which part of the industry they want to fit into and endeavour to progress their studies in the desired subject area.

Appendices

Useful Websites

ACI – The Financial Markets Association	www.aciforex.com
Bank of International Settlements	www.bis.org
British Bankers Association	www.bba.org.com
Bloomberg	www.bloomberg.com
Dun and Bradstreet	www.dnb.com
EBRD	www.ebrd.com
Eurex	www.eurexchange.com
Euromoney Publications	www.euromoney.com
Euronext	www.euronext.com
European Bank for Reconstruction and Development	www.ebrd.com
European Central Bank	www.ecb.int
Financial Times	www.ft.com
Fitch	www.fitchibca.com
Fix Protocol	www.fixprotocol.org
International Monetary Fund	www.imf.org
ISMA	www.isma.org
London Stock Exchange	www.londonstockexchange.com/
Moody's Investor Services	www.moodys.com
Reuters	www.reuters.com
SWIFT	www.swift.com
Standard and Poor's	www.standardandpoors.com
The Bank of England	www.bankofengland.com
The Economist	www.economist.com
Thomson Financial	www.thomson.com
World Bank	www.worldbank.com

Specialist Recruitment Agencies

Robert Half	www.roberthalf.co.uk
Michael Page	www.michaelpage.com
McGregor Boyall	www.mcgregor-boyall.com
Badenoch and Clark	www.badenochandclark.com
Robert Walters	www.robertwalters.com
Banking People	www.banking-people.com
Aston Carter	www.astoncarter.co.uk
Rule Financial	www.rulefinancial.com
Hatstand	www.hatstand-ltd.com
Hudson	www.hudson.com
Lorien	www.lorien.co.uk
752 Solutions	www.752Solutions.com
Cititec	www.cititec.com
Anson McCade	www.ansonmccade.com
Oldbury Howard	www.oldburyhoward.com
Joslin Rowe	www.joslinrowe.com
JM Contracts	www.jmpeople.com
Allison International	www.allisoninternational.com
Project Partners	www.projpartners.com
James Harvard Financial	www.jamesharvardfinancial.com

References

About BIS, available from www.bis.org/about/index.htm

About Bloomberg, available form http://about.bloomberg.com/about/index.html

About Data and News, available from www.cqg.com.

About Euroclear, available from www.euroclear.com/wps/portal

About FISD, available from www.FISD.net

About Thomson Financial, available from www.thomson.com/about

A Primer on the Forex Market, available from www.investopedia.com/articles/trading.

Amos, G. and Nolan, D. (2001) *Mastering Treasury Office Operations*. Pearson Education Limited.

Andes, C. and Beck, K.(2004) *Extreme Programming Explained*. Addison-Wesley

Bank of International Settlements. (April 2003) *Overview of the New Basel Capital Accord,*. pp 5.

Bentley, K. (1997) *Prince 2: A Practical Handbook*. Butterworth–Heinemann Ltd.

Chaplin, G. (2005) *Credit Derivatives*. Wiley Finance.

Chisholm, A. (2002) *An Introduction to Capital Markets*. Wiley Finance.

CLS Shareholders, available from www.cls-services.com/whoswho/shareholders

Deloitte Financial Services (2006) *Global Financial Services Outlook*, pp 2–16.

Endur – A world where financial and physical solutions always mesh, available from
      www.olf.com/energy/solutions/endur.

Findur – A world where financial and physical solutions always mesh, available from
      www.olf.com/energy/solutions/findur.

Fight, A. (2004) *Syndicated Lending*. Elsevier Butterworth-Heinemann Ltd.

"Fixed Income". Wikipedia: The Free Encyclopedia. 30 August 2006.
      http://en.wikipedia.org/wiki/Fixed_income

Goldman Sachs Second Quarter Results, available from
      http://www2.goldmansachs.com/our_firm/media_center/articles, International Monetary
      Fund. (2002) *Credit Derivatives in Emerging Markets*, pp 5.

IBM Business Consulting Service. (2006) Launch assess, wait. A practical guide to preparing for
      MiFID, pp 3, 11.

Illyina, A., Mathieson, D., Roldos, J. (2004) *Emerging Local Securities and Derivatives Market*.
      International Monetary Fund (IMF).

"Investment Banking". Wikipedia: The Free Encyclopedia. 30 Aug 2006.
      http://en.wikipedia.org/wiki/Investment_banking.

JPMorgan Chase Earnings Release, available from http://investor.shareholder.com/jpmorgan-
      chase/earnings.

Kessler, R. and Williams. (2002) *Pair Programming Illuminated*. Addison-Wesley.

Kit, E. (1995) *Software Testing in the Real World*. Addison-Wesley.

L'Habitant, F.S. (2003). *An introduction to Capital Markets by Hedge Funds: Myths and Limits*.
      Wiley Finance.

Liaw, K. (2006) *The Business of Investment banking*. Wiley.

McInytre, H. (2004) *Straight Through Processing*. Summit Group Press.

MDDL Overview, available from www.mddl.org/overview.

MDDL: The Liberator of Market Data, available from www.dmreview.co/editorial.

Merrill Lynch Corporate Snapshot, available from www.ml.com.

Morgan Stanley Reports Second Quarter Results, available from
      www.morganstanley.com/about/ir/shareholder/

129

MSCI A Leading Global Benchmark Provider, available from www.msci.com/overview/index.

MSCI Index Definition, available from www.msci.com/equity/indexdesc.

Multibank platforms, available from www.londonfx.co.uk/ecn.

Reuters Tick Capture Engine Past, Present and Precise, available from www.Reuters.com.

Schuh, P. (2004) *Integrating Agile Development in the Real World*. Charles River Media.

Shamal, S. (2003) *A Foreign Exchange Primer*. John Wiley and Sons Ltd.

Spot Trading, available from www.londonfx.co.uk/trading.

Teasedale, A. (2003) *An Introduction to Fixed Income Securities*. Yield Curve Publishing.

Volume of shares traded on London Stock Exchange, available from
www.londonstockexchange.com.

What is FPML? available from www.fpml.org/news/factsheet.

Why Trade Contract for difference? available from http://www.contracts-for-difference.com/trade-cfds.

Index

Page numbers in italic indicate figures or tables.

Index compiled by Marian Anderson.

About Essvale Corporation

Essvale Corporation Limited is a consultancy, training and publishing firm. The firm is focused on fostering the alignment of the IT industry with the business community and promoting the development of innovative ideas.

At Essvale our mission is to "innovate, create and deliver".

The following are the range of services offered by Essvale Corporation Limited:

IT and Business Consulting

We offer consulting services in IT and business in investment banking, asset management and retail banking. The asset classes we cover are as follows:

- FX
- Fixed Income
- Equities
- Cash

IT consulting services we offer on software development projects include:

- Application Development
- Test Analysis
- Application Support
- Project Management
- Business Analysis

For more information on our consulting services please send an email to consult@essvale.com.

Training

We offer training services to clients as part of our consulting services and also partner training schools to offer on-site training courses. Our unique approach to training is what sets us apart as we are constantly developing innovative training initiatives.

We are currently in the process of launching our unique brand of Bizle training materials. These course materials are created in an "off-the-shelf" format, but could be customised to suit different regional markets and industry sectors.

After selling course materials to clients we offer train-the-trainers courses to ensure that their trainers can deliver the courses as designed.

137

We have also devised a certification programme for our courses using our unique points system.

For more information on training please send an email to: training@essvale.com.

Our Vision

The vision of the firm in the near future is to be at the forefront of technical authoring and rapidly expanding our publishing and consulting capabilities. We intend to create alliances with established and up-and-coming application vendors in the financial services market space to expand our service offerings in the implementation and support of business-critical systems in this market.

About the Bizle Professional Series

Bizle is the first of its kind that seeks to bridge the knowledge gap between IT professionals and the business community. Any professional that has worked in IT can attest to the disparity which is plaguing the workplace in terms of the gulf in business knowledge.

IT has to be more business aligned and this is more evident with the increasing dependence by the "business" on it. Application vendors, in investment banking for instance, are surpassing themselves in getting business-critical systems into the market for trading, compliance and risk management only to realise that the in-house IT staff and contractors are not adequately skilled to deploy and maintain these systems.

This situation has to change and quickly too; technology is shaping the operations and reliance on it will be even greater in the longer term.

Bizle publications aim to be at the forefront of these radical changes and there is ongoing effort and research at Essvale Corporation Limited to achieve these goals.

Introducing Bizle.biz

Bizle.biz is the first online portal dedicated to the alignment of IT and business. When fully operational, Bizle will be the reference point for IT students and professionals that want to keep abreast of issues concerning IT and the alignment with the business community. It will also provide answers to "on-the-job" queries that professionals might have during the course of their everyday tasks.

Bizle.biz will have the following features:

- IT jobs adverts partitioned into the industry sectors to allow both candidates and advertisers to tailor their job requirements
- Recommended Books
- Industry News
- 'Ask' support service
- Glossary of Terms
- Forum
- Content in different languages.